I0025616

LETS
GO
PUBLISH

Defeating America's Career Politicians

Corrupt career politicians are killing America

Refresh your knowledge of the specific rights granted to all Americans.

Americans who hate corruption should love what the founders gave us in The Bill of Rights. Learn about your rights and freedoms by reading The Bill of Rights.

After understanding the Constitution, this is the best thing you can do to understand your role in assuring our great form of government. Our nation, our freedom and our liberties are being attacked today by corrupt left-leaning anti-American politicians. This book is one of the tools needed to stop them.

It does not get any better than reading a crisp copy of The Bill of Rights by James Madison. It is the best means for anybody who is reengaging with America or to give to a friend or relative who needs a nudge to understand what would be lost without our Constitution and Bill of Rights… or worst yet, without America as founded.

Even if you learned civics years ago, knowledge of which, by the way, is hard to find today, more than likely you are unsure of what America offers in the way of rights, and powers, and the duties for Americans to achieve them. This book has been written as a first step to help you be better prepared to react to the over-reach of corrupt politicians at the highest levels of government. Know your rights or lose your rights!

Without the knowledge that you can gain easily in this book, for example, you might think that your representatives in Congress hold all the cards, and that mum is the word. You may think that you can speak freely only in the free speech zones of American universities. If you feel pressure to behave in a politically-correct fashion, this book is your first antidote to coming out of the funk and the group-think, and thinking again for yourself.

Today more than ever with the government of our past president attempting to regain control of the people, and his leftover deep state officials attempting to un-elect our duly elected president it is a necessity for Americans to know that we run the government and the government does not run us. Americans are not born knowing our rights. Yet, we must know our rights and the protections built into the basic framework of our government formed by the US Constitution and the Bill of Rights or it will be easy to lose them all. Why did we wait so long to find this book?

Just because powerful elite officials, who are part of the corrupt establishment in both political Parties choose to ignore our rights and freedoms does not mean we must endure tyranny. The first step of course is to understand the most basic written precepts in the Constitution and the fully described Bill of Ten written by Patriot President James Madison well before he ascended to the presidency of the USA. Madison would tell you that today ladies & gentlemen, reading this book is a must.

BRIAN W. KELLY

Title: Defeating America's Career Politicians
Copyright © 2017 Brian W. Kelly
Publisher: Brian P. Kelly
Author Brian W. Kelly

Published by: .... LETS GO PUBLISH!
Editor .... Brian P. Kelly
Email: .... info@letsgopublish.com
Web site.. www.letsgopublish.com
Cover Designer .... Brian W. Kelly

Library of Congress Copyright Information Pending

ISBN Information: The International Standard Book Number (ISBN) is a unique machine-readable identification number, which marks any book unmistakably. The ISBN is the clear standard in the book industry. 159 countries and territories are officially ISBN members. The Official ISBN for this book is on the outside cover:

ISBN: **978-1-947402-11-9**

The price for this work is: **$14.95 USD**
10 9 8 7 6 5 4 3 2 1
Release Date: October 2017

Dedication

To the entire Kelly Family.
(My father's side of the family)

They have all stood there with me and I with them, as we seek the truth and continue our fight for our freedoms.

The gentlemen Kelly's on this list fought in World War II or the Korean War. We thank them deeply for their service.

Uncle Mart, Uncle Ed, Aunt Marie, Aunt Catherine, Aunt Helen, Uncle Pat, Uncle Mike, Uncle Phil, Uncle Joe, and Uncle Johnnie

God bless them all!

Acknowledgments

In every book that I write or edit, I publicly acknowledged all of the help that I have received from many sources. Some of these wonderful people are still on earth and others have made their way to heaven.

I would like to thank many people for helping me in this effort. I appreciate all the help that I received in putting this book together, along with the 126 other books from the past.

My printed acknowledgments were once so large that book readers needed to navigate too many pages to get to page one of the text. To permit me more flexibility, I put my acknowledgment list online at www.letsgopublish.com. The list of acknowledgments continues to grow. Believe it or not, it once cost about a dollar more to print each book.

Thank you all on the big list in the sky and God bless you all for your help.

Please check out www.letsgopublish.com to read the latest version of my heartfelt acknowledgments updated for this book. Thank you all!

In this book, I received some extra special help from many avid America supporters including Bruce Ikeda, Dennis Grimes, Gerry Rod ski, Wily Ky Eyely, Angel Irene McKeown Kelly, Angel Edward Joseph Kelly Sr., Angel Edward Joseph Kelly Jr., Ann Flannery, Angel James Flannery Sr., Mary Daniels, Bill Daniels, Robert Gary Daniels, Angel Sarah Janice Daniels, Angel Punkie Daniels, Joe Kelly, Diane Kelly, Brian P. Kelly, Mike P. Kelly, Katie P. Kelly, Angel Ben Kelly, and Budmund (Buddy) Arthur Kelly.

Preface

Sometimes I do ask myself, "Do we Americans deserve any rights?" If you listen to the popular press and to the liberal communist progressives, who are overwhelming our government today, you will conclude they think the answer is "no." They are convinced we would do better under their control.

And, so to help their end game, they have rigged all elections against the people by providing a corrupt system of electing our representatives. These "ministers of the people" do everything but minister to the people as the rewards from political corruption are too lucrative to turn down.

The top rung of the political ladder know that they would do better by shutting out the people for even in communism, there are some "elites" at the top who gain the spoils. And, of course, in communism, there is no pesky Congress or other notions that the people expect any sort of power. It is a great deal for the officials left after the proletariats execute the purge or the donor class shows their appreciation.

Sometimes our current corrupt officials forget, however. that there are more of us than them so please do not get hoodwinked believing any of their spiel. The colonists beat the heavily armed English because they outnumbered the English and they were fighting for their home country. Once the people are back in this game, knowing our rights, nobody will be able to take them away.

I have a one sentence speech that might fly in Central America but it should not fly in America once real Americans understand what they would be giving up: "Why should Americans have lives that are nice when the rest of the world is suffering? Ask yourself, what part of your personal America are you willing to give up for nameless, faceless, people who could care a hoot about whether you live or die.

That's what it is all about today, folks. I hope that is why you are reading this book, written to counteract the influences of corrupt dirty politicians using rights written by one of our greatest founders, James Madison.

Why is the US press and the bulk of government workers so anti-American? Can you figure that one out? Maybe they should take up residence someplace else and torment another group of people.

Early Americans fought for our rights and later Americans fought to preserve them. Communists were never interested in protecting our rights in the beginning, the middle, and surely not now when many non-thinking Americans are prepared to hand our country over to the corrupt people in our government who represent them.

So, what rhetoric would you expect from those that espouse an ideology that says government should take from you so that Joe Bloe down the street should never have to worry about working? Joe Bloe will never have any rights other than the short term right to not work for his meager welfare payments.

Since neither Communism nor communism has ever worked in any country, you and I know that life won't always be sweet for Joe Bloe and Mary Bloe. However, neither Joe nor Mary know it and they would not believe you if you read the history of the world to them 100 or more times.

American rights are not a gift. They were not donated to Americans by anybody. Many Americans fought and many died for independence from the tyranny of England as well as in World Wars and other wars. America was always on the side of right and our great country still is on the side of right.

Once our own independence, freedoms, and liberties were gained from the bloodshed. The objective always was to keep the rest of the world safe and permit the whole world to live as well as it could in safety. America is a good country. America and Americans have helped our neighbors across the world from our founding.

The graves of our sons and fathers and grandfathers with tombstones stretched across the world are vivid proof of our kindness as a country and our desire to help all the people of the world to become or to remain free. Don't let the *Blame America First* crowd talk down America while you are in the room. America and Americans deserve better.

Americans should not have to apologize to anybody. We should have no guilt. Yet, our bought and paid for corrupt press and our current government would love to ram tyranny down our throats by telling us we are bad people. Please don't buy any of it. We are not bad people. We are exceptional people. Nobody has ever done in the existence of recorded history as much as America and Americans have done for our fellow man in America and across the world.

If you choose to wait until a Democrat, a progressive, a Marxist, or a communist says something good about America, you will be waiting a lifetime. Think about that while you consider if big government is really good for the people. Think again, please. Big government is good for big shots, big money, big corporations, big unions, a big corrupt press, and other big thinkers who hate America.

It has been 240 plus years since the United States, our country, achieved its independence. Along with independence, we the people, through the grace of our founders, earned freedom and liberty. Nobody has a right to demean US for that and nobody can take it away.

Ironically, there are some in America who espouse the liberal progressive Marxist ideology despite its demands that they give up on America. They are fully ready to blame America first for everything. They hate you and I and I bet you they do not even know why! They probably do not like anybody including themselves and their "best friends."

Ironically, here we are, 240 plus years after the Constitution and we still cannot get these people to agree that freedom is a good thing. Yet without freedom, they could not operate their clandestine socialist works in our country. As far as I am concerned it is OK if they all left town and went on to their favorite suppressed country to practice their ideology. They hurt America every day.

Though all is not perfect in America, the principles of the Constitution and the Bill of Rights are so sound and so powerful that even a knave politician cannot bring us under. The big concern of course is that if we all or at least if most of us do not smarten up, things will get a lot worse. I suspect that this is why you have chosen to read this book.

Our ailments have been large and growing in the Obama years. Taxes are still too high; elected officials are out of touch; government is too big; spending is out of control; the new healthcare program is a train wreck; the federal government is incompetent; the people have no voice in government; too many people are too lazy to hold government accountable; too many officials are on the take, and worse than that, the list of ailments is growing, not shortening.

Things are happening that are lawless. In 2014, for example, the leader of the free world, without the required permission from the US Congress, traded five terrorists for a POW who had deserted his unit in Afghanistan. On camera, his father praised Allah and that too was difficult to understand considering the negotiations with the Taliban had been fruitless for years.

Meanwhile a former marine, a documented hero, while negotiations for the traitor were going on, was rotting in a Mexican jail. Why? Because the leader of the free world at the time, would not pick up his phone and his pen and demand that this patriot be released.

Instead after a few more months of punishment for him being in the military, the President would have an epiphany and emerge in a political ceremony claiming he did not know about the Marine's plight. Then, he would take credit for his release. That's how it was back in the days of the last eight years. I trusted more but it is tough to trust a liar.

Your intention no doubt in learning about the structure of America and its most fundamental laws, especially the Bill of Rights in choosing to read this book is to help you understand why all this is happening. Thank you. That is why my dad wrote this book. I am betting that more sooner than later, you will better understand our great country and our great form of government—at least before the bad guys take it away.

This book is the best starter book for anybody wanting to know how things really area and at the same time to refresh their knowledge or learn about the government of the United States of America. Those wanting to be better prepared to react to the over-reach of today's corrupt politicians at the highest levels of government will find this book gives them their answers. Without the knowledge that you can gain easily in this book, for example, you might not understand your rights. Then what?

This might cause you to unknowingly be convinced by socialist progressives in the government or influenced by the government that you have no rights, and that you have no freedoms, and all of your permissions to act come from the government itself.

If you have been paying attention to what was going on in the prior administration, you know that as a country, we are in trouble. We have a busted economy, high unemployment, no jobs, and our basic rights to freedoms such as speech, religion, the press, and our right-to-bear-arms are being impinged upon. The founders saw it as a civic duty for Americans to pay attention to our government so that we can avoid being chumps and being snookered by crooked politicians.

There are more issues than just those noted above, and we better fix them quickly while we still have a Constitution and a Bill of Rights and a fine new President upon which to lean.

We are on the same side in this battle for the Constitution, the Bill of Rights, and for the survival of America. Together we can all help. We first must understand what is going on and we then must understand our rights as delivered in the Declaration of Independence, The Constitution, and the Bill of Rights.

My concern is that when we all wake up from our deep fog, there may be no Bill of Rights or Constitution left for our progeny. We will have blown it for sure if that is permitted to happen.

In this book, Brian W. Kelly unabashedly recommends that we stop trusting government since it is clearly not working for our best interests. The sooner we can understand the threat from the left, the sooner we can move on to solving the problem for our values, our country, and our freedom.

The smarter we are, the more chance we have for success. Understanding America's founding and the founding documents, especially the Constitution and The Bill of Rights, is a sure way to become an American forever. I know you love America as I do.

Your author continually monitors what is happening to our government and he has written extensively on the major problems our country faces. Brian W. Kelly is one of America's most outspoken and eloquent conservative spokesmen. He is the author of *America 4 Dummmie*s, *The Constitution 4 Dummmies*, *Sol Bloom's Epoch Story of the Constitution*, *No Amnesty! No Way! Saving America*, *Taxation Without Representation*, *Obama's Seven Deadly Sins*, *Kill the EPA!*, *Jobs! Jobs! Jobs! The Federalist Papers* by the Framers, and many other patriotic books. All books are available at amazon.com/author/brianwkelly.

Like many Americans, Brian W Kelly, my dad, is fed up with stifling socialist progressive Marxists in the top seats in Washington. They place the needs of everybody else in front of the needs of Americans. Like many Americans, Kelly is shocked at how brazen the Obama administration was in ignoring our Constitution and our Bill of Rights! This had to be stopped. In November 2016, the threats ended. We are all pleased with the new president's actions so far and we ask his fellow Republicans in Congress to get on the stick and make sure you support our President or you will be gone.

Brian W. Kelly has read the founding documents, the underlying intelligence reports, and he has researched and written about such topics for years. Brian has written one hundred twenty-six books and hundreds of patriotic articles. He is deeply concerned about how intolerable the results of poor government policy can be within our neighborhoods and our lives. His comprehensible and sane recommendations in this book are explained in detail within the covers of this soon-to-be classic edition.

You are going to love this book, designed by an American for Americans. Few books are must-read but *The Bill of Rights by Founder James Madison* will quickly be at the top of America's most read list.

Sincerely,

Brian P. Kelly, Editor

Table of Contents

About the Author

Brian W. Kelly retired as an Assistant Professor in the Business Information Technology (BIT) program at Marywood University, where he also served as the IBM i and midrange systems technical advisor to the IT faculty. Kelly has designed, developed, and taught many college and professional courses. He is also a contributing technical editor to a number of IT industry magazines, including "The Four Hundred" and "Four Hundred Guru" published by IT Jungle. On the Patriotic side, you once could find a patriotic Kelly article at www.conservativeactionalerts.com. This site no longer functions but the articles are still hosted at www.brianwkelly.com

Kelly is a former IBM Senior Systems Engineer and he has been a candidate for US Congress and the US Senate from Pennsylvania. He has an active information technology consultancy. He is the author of 127 books and numerous articles. Kelly is a frequent speaker at National Conferences, and other technical conferences. Ask him to speak at your next TEA Party rally! You might be surprised!

Over the past twenty years, Brian Kelly has become one of America's most outspoken and eloquent conservative protagonists. Besides this book, America 4 Dummmies, and The Constitution 4 Dummmies, Kelly is also the author of No Amnesty! No Way! Taxation Without Representation, and many other patriotic books. Books are available at www.amazon.com/author/Brianwkelly

Endorsed by the Independence Hall Tea Party in 2010, Kelly, a conservative Democrat, ran for Congress against a 13-term Democrat and, took no campaign contributions, spent enough to buy signs and T-shirts, and as a virtual unknown, he captured 17% of the vote—

www.briankellyforcongress.com. Kelly then supported Republican challenger Lou Barletta, a conservative leader on immigration policy, and helped him win a resounding victory in the general election. Barletta is now a Senatorial Candidate in PA running against Democrat Bob Casey, Jr.

Chapter 1 Can the people win in the battle for America?

Americans who hate corruption should love their rights

The game is rigged. We all know it and we talk about it a lot. It is disheartening as nobody seems to have the answer. Seventy-five percent of Americans believe that the government is corrupt, period, and the trajectory for this opinion is on the rise. Less and less Americans trust that their government is working for them.

When you think of the system being rigged, we all recall Donald Trump more than hinting that the electoral process was rigged for Hillary. Bernie Sanders may also have something to say about that.

Trump took a lot of heat from the press when he acknowledged the underlying truth of American politics that every politician takes money from anybody who will legally give it to them. Many take it from any source.

Remember Candidate Trump's words at the Republican debate: "Most of the people on this stage I've given to, just so you understand, a lot of money … I give to everybody. When they call, I give" he admitted. "And do you know what? When I need something from them two years later, three years later, I call them, they are there for me. And that's a broken system." It sure is

Looking at newscasts affirms the opinion of a high corruption index as not a week goes by without a media exposé of yet another corruption scandal involving a politician, corporate executive, a simple opportunist or even a local landlord or businessman. We have a culture of corruption in America and it is everywhere. They smaller a citizen stands on the totem pole, the tougher it is to get a fair shot at anything that touches government hands.

Michelle Malkin wrote a book titled: Culture of Corruption: Obama and His Team of Tax Cheats, Crooks, and Cronies. It highlights the last eight years of one corrupt act after another.

Anne rated the book four stars and admits that she learned so much that she got sick: "The bigger government gets, the more corruption there is. I think it's even worse with this administration because no one but people like Michelle are looking at what is really going on. The book made me feel sick. I knew that there was corruption, but I really didn't know the extent. How's that hope and change working???"

Another reader of this book rated it five stars. Her name is Charlotte. She wrote an insightful comment that is worth your time: "This highly documented and footnoted work of investigative journalism will do nothing short of quell any illusions that we have a man of integrity in the White House. The depth and breadth of this Administration's exposed corruption and cronyism will surely turn the stomach of all Americans who value honesty, integrity, and their hard-earned taxpayer dollars.

Written with wit and attention to detail, just one of the many disturbing revelations of the book is how our tax dollars are being used to fund this super-charade of "transparency" and the "end of business as usual." Beyond the Obama administration, Malkin further catalogues the intrigue and craftiness of the Clinton Team, and other players. It is impossible to refute the facts, and they come hard and fast in Malkin's work. She shows the same insightfulness, intelligence and quick-wit in her writing that she demonstrates in her live interviews, making what otherwise might be a dull parade of fact after gut-wrenching fact a lively romp through the swamp of corruption that is the current political machine."

Despite the corruption, even though we are now in an era in American History in which the game seems rigged because the game is rigged, unlike Hollywood celebrities who hate Trump, none of my friends are packing to leave. Corruption has not become acceptable to Americans but we cannot deny it. As noted, a growing proportion of the Americans acknowledge that the game is rigged, that government and corporations are — individually and colluding together – corrupt institutions.

Fighting back is something to which many Americans are unaccustomed. Yet we are beginning to boil about the situation and many of us have begun to act. You are reading this book, for example, because understanding the facts about citizens' rights as presented in the Constitution, and the Bill of Rights are more and more important to all Americans wanting to regain a fair playing field. There is lots we can do but most of it is not easy.

It begins with not trusting government employees and officials—the higher up the least trustworthy. The second step is to pay attention and the third step is to learn your rights. The fourth step is to take positive action to end corruption. The first test to see if Americans have the mettle to end political corruption was when Donald Trump beat seventeen Republicans as well as overwhelming favorite Hillary Clinton to become our 45th President. Many are hoping this will be the start of something good. It shows Americans are fed up with corruption and are ready to take action rather than sit around and wait for things to happen.

It surely is not tough living in the 21st century for most things compared to the founding times and the centuries since then. However, the government back then was formed of, for, and by the people who were mostly smart honest patriots who lived and died or almost died in a revolution to provide Americans liberty and freedom. Though there is always a level of corruption when men interact with men, today, corruption in our government has become the order of the day. It is no longer the exception.

During our founding, colonists, feeling oppression from their European heritage countries chose to leave the comforts of their home country to go to the new world. Rather than put up with the deprivation of life's natural freedoms and liberties, many gladly signed, often indenturing themselves to established wealthier colonists for a year or two to take the seven-week journey to the new world. They came to America assured that the knaves that had corrupted their home countries would be far away. After a lot of struggles, hard work, and finally, a revolution, the people in the new world were free, and life was much better.

How to form a government was the first major issue for the post-revolution elites in America. They were smart enough to know that for the new country to succeed, a just government needed to be framed and established that would be strong against potential foes from other lands. Just winning the revolution was not enough. The former colonists needed to figure out how to keep America free.

As they searched for the right form of government, the founders found four qualities that needed to be included in our government. They borrowed from wherever they could and the Roman and Greek models were often part of their evaluation. They founded our nation as a Republic.

Four special qualities have distinguished our republican government from ancient Athens forward. These include 1. the sovereignty of the people, 2. a sense of the common good, 3. a government dedicated to the commonwealth, and 3, a resistance to corruption. How could such things be achieved by a bunch of folks who had just come over on the boat? Among other things, necessity and raw determination are the answers.

When we examine our US republic against the standards established for republics from ancient times, especially in our current times, we would universally declare that the American Republic in which we live today is massively corrupt.

From Plato and Aristotle forward, corruption was meant to describe actions and decisions that put a narrow, special, or personal interest ahead of the interest of the public or commonwealth. Corruption did not have to stoop to money under the table, vote buying, or even renting out the Lincoln bedroom. But, let's face it none of that helped the regular people trust the government in the late decades of the twentieth century and the early decades of the 21st century.

The corruption became so thick, the people knew their sacred US had been compromised but had no direct solution as most of their remedies from the Constitution had become in one way or another corrupted. The best vestige of an honest past was that even the corrupt could not figure out how to rig elections with impunity. In the governing of the US Republic, corruption was self-interest placed above the interest of all—the public interest. For a time, the people were able to thwart corruption by voting out the few that were corrupt. Today, we are challenged as Abraham to find just a few honest politicians. Do you remember scriptures:

For example, you may recall when Abraham begged for the corrupt city of Sodom. His words:

25 "Far be it from You to do such a thing, to slay the righteous with the wicked, so that the righteous and the wicked are treated alike. Far be it from You! Shall not the Judge of all the earth deal justly?"

26 So the LORD said, "If I find in Sodom fifty righteous within the city, then I will spare the whole place on their account."

27 And Abraham replied, "Now behold, I have ventured to speak to the Lord, although I am but dust and ashes…."

How many times did Abraham go back because the people were corrupt and did not want to stop their sinning?

Let me repeat that in the governing of the US Republic, corruption was self-interest placed above the interest of all––the public interest. By that standard, few would even consider contesting that our government is corrupt. It had gotten so bad that Americans who were mostly unaware of their rights, felt they had “a mystery right” to take on the government. Let me ask you. Do you think any adult living recently can seriously doubt that our republic, our government, is corrupt?

From the middle times in our republic, there have been lots of issues that smelled like corruption but yet we survived. There have been Teapot Domes and financial scandals of one kind or another throughout our nation’s history. There has never been a time, like today, however, when the government of the United States was so perversely and systematically dedicated to special interests, earmarks, side deals, log-rolling, vote-trading, and sweetheart deals of one kind or another than the times in which we now live.

Who could tell me with a straight face and some facts, what brought us to this? Look around you. If you thought about running for a major office, would you be able to do so if somebody with a preferred person backing them wanted to do you in?

John Edwards talked about two Americas. He was right because of the massive corruption in public offices. You know that we have created a sinister system combining staggering campaign costs, political contributions, political action committees, special interest payments for access, and, most of all, the rise of the lobbying class. Are you, as a potential future candidate, part of any of these forms of strength to help you ride to a campaign victory? More than likely not! When you run for office, you will hear otherwise honest men suggest that you take the money so you can get elected. Unfortunately, once a greasy-palm gets its fill it is often back for more from the trough when the palm is empty.

Probably the worst thing that happened to our esteemed elected is lobbyists, who get paid to turn simple people from farm countries into millionaires. Worse than that, the huge army of lobbyists that started relatively small in the mid-twentieth century has now grown to massive battalions of law firms and lobbying firms of the right, left, and an amalgam of both. Regular Joe's in America cannot play and win in such a high stakes game. But, if we can reject their self-serving rhetoric, we can vote the bad guys to Kingdom come.

How many times have you said or heard somebody else say how nice it would be if only a good man would come forth to become a candidate for office—for any office. Nobody, even the dishonest, find dishonesty attractive. So, mostly everybody has a great disdain for dishonesty, even if they are the most dishonest of all. Talk is cheap. Action takes guts.

But action in the electoral process never happens for the people unless the individual candidate is honest and has money. We know that money is the root of all evil, but we also know that nobody can take a step towards a helpful political position without somebody else's money if they are not financial endowed to begin with.

Knowing this, we still do long for the perfect candidate to beat the knaves but in reality, even if one showed up, the dollars spent on other candidates might even convince the best of us to look the other way to the lead candidate with major backing. If Joe across the street is the best man. Would we back him if our political friends press us? And, so, in the end, we get the government we deserve. Few of us are willing to fight for the regular guy to become a representative of the people even though they claim to long fir such a person. What a shame!

Once a good guy comes to Washington and does his or her time for the people, when they leave their roles as representatives, that gargantuan, if not reptilian, industry takes on board former members of the House and the Senate and their personal and committee staffs. And they all get fabulously rich, and nobody cares or so it seems, and nobody just eats cake.

I wish it were not so but in recent years, this development has been so insidious that it now goes without notice. The people are held in submission by politicians who promise and promise and who do deliver simple amenities from the US treasury. Sometimes these amenities buy off the regular class who are not paying attention.

We might call this quid-pro-quo bribery from the esteemed class. The key word is access—access to those with power. In exchange for a few moments of the senator or representative's time and many more moments of his committee staff's time, fund-raising events with the promise of tens, even hundreds, of thousands of dollars are delivered and the donor waits until the representative can deliver the quid pro quo, which always comes. Simple regular citizens are given lip service and mostly have no chance in hades when running for office against the corrupt monied class.

Corruption in a federated republic such as ours operates vertically as well as horizontally. Seeing how business is conducted in Washington, it did not take long for governors of both parties across the country to subscribe to the special-interest state. A few hundred thousand in salary does not compare to the rewards of corruption paid by the lobbyists and other special donors to departing officials whose terms are over. A few million for lobbyists and special interests is a "hell" of a lot better than a government pension. Having both is an even better deal! That, my friends are corruption to the nth degree.

Neither party is exempt from corruption. As a conservative Democrat, I naturally believe Dems are corrupt because I have seen them in action close up. Republican members of Congress have been aggravating their voters by wimpiness and inaction. The one-time loyalists have begun to understand that Republicans are actually Democrats without having the names. Neither party respects the people anymore.

For example, at the state level, both the Republican and Democratic governors' associations formed "social welfare" organizations composed of wealthy interests and corporate executives to raise money for their respective parties in exchange for close, personal access to individual governors, governors who almost surely could render executive decisions favorable to those corporate interests. The reason you are so anxious to get to the next paragraph is not because of what it contains since I wrote it and know. But, it is because you already know that access pays off big time for politicians that you and others continually reelect. We have to stop doing that.

A series of judicial decisions enabled these "social welfare" groups, who were supposedly barred from political activity, to channel virtually unlimited amounts of funds to governors, senators, and representatives in exchange for access, which is the political coin of the realm in this corrupted republic. They get away with it because the press is on their side and partakes in the booty and they do their dirty work out of sight of the American people. When we the people learn about such indiscretions, we are more inclined to forgive than we should.

When anybody chooses to serve the people, they are blocked. Even the New York Times commented that "the stealthy form of political corruption known as 'dark money' now fully permeates governor's offices around the country, allowing corporations to push past legal barriers and gather enormous influence." We use the term "governor" but all political animals are subject to the same notions when access to power is the desired end.

Frustrated, irate discussions of this legalized corruption are met regularly in the corrupt Washington media with a shrug. So, what? Who cares? Didn't we just have dinner with that lobbyist for the IT industry, or the Steam Fitters' union, or the airline industry at that well-known journalist's house only two nights ago? Fine lady, and she used to be the chairman of one of those powerful committees. I gather she is using her Rolodex rather skillfully on behalf of her new clients.

Is any of this illegal? Illegal? Not at all. It is simply smart . . . and so charming.

There is little wonder that Americans of the right and many in the middle are apoplectic at their government and absolutely, and rightly, convinced that the game of government is rigged in favor of the elite and the powerful players in the corrupt political game.

Occupiers see even more wealth rising to the top at the expense of the poor and the middle class. And Tea Partiers believe their tax dollars are going to well-organized welfare parasites and government bureaucrats.

And, of course, the ultimate victims of the corruption of the democratic process are not defeated candidates and parties but America's citizens. Try getting an honest government today. Does it matter? It sure does but what common man can fight the power of such organized corruption.

Perhaps Supreme Court Justices, if we can put them above many of ourselves as bastions of goodness and truth, should have to experience a corrupted election process firsthand to recognize a hollowed-out democracy. As a guy I know once lamented, one who watched Watergate through the eyes of a press that wanted to unseat a president, it is surely not pleasant to find people under surveillance by the press, guilty or not guilty, to find your taxes audited, and to experience all the dirty tricks in the book. All this happened to many including presidents and presidential hopefuls.

As recently as the 2014 election, the facts documented this government of influence by secrecy: "More than half of the general election advertising aired by outside groups in the battle for control of Congress," according to the New York Times, "has come from organizations that disclose little or nothing about their donors, a flood of secret money that is now at the center of a debate over the line between free speech and corruption." How is that good for America or Americans? It's like we need a rebuilt RICO act to tame errant politicians across the entire nation.

The five prevailing Supreme Court justices, held that a legal entity called a corporation has First Amendment rights of free speech, while Unions were tacitly given full capability to donate to whom it may. How can John Q Public fight against the money and power of Wall Street, Big Industry, and Big Labor,

With a huge budget, think how much good any organization can do in the campaign finance arena. Why pay for a senator or congresswoman here or there when you can buy an entire committee that gives you if you are a lobbyist, full access to all? Take them all out to dinner with huge perquisites and secret gifts—even cash! As a legislator, or powerful lobbyist with the connections, think of the banks that you can bail out of any issue, and the remunerations that might come your way.

The lobbying business is now big business. It is no longer about a small handout for a favor. It is not just about votes up or down on particular measures that may emerge in Congress or policies made in the White House. It is about setting whole agendas, deciding what should and should not be brought up for hearings and legislation. It is about writing the laws rather than let the congressional staffers get that done.

America in our hallowed halls has gone way beyond mere vote buying now. The converging Influence World represents nothing less than an unofficial but enormously powerful fourth branch of government. It is a fifth branch if we consider the press. Americans must use their rights to fight this assault on our freedoms and liberties—assaults surely have come with more coming soon. It may seem like it can't be done but all things are possible.

Remember the steps to de-lousing America. I will repeat them as they are important to getting the rehab of America done correctly. It begins with not trusting government employees and officials—the higher up the least trustworthy. The second step is to pay attention and the third step is to learn your rights as you are doing with this book and others. The fourth step is to take positive action to end corruption. Don't be a chump.

To whom is any branch of government accountable? Who can assure that the Congress, for example, really wants to represent the people and not the special interests?

Who sets the agenda for Congress's rising army of influence marketers? How easy will it be to not only go from a Senatorial or Congressional office to a lucrative lobbying job but to also gain buckets of cash as the reward. Perhaps even more importantly and more seductive and seditious for America—how about a quick road from a lucrative lobbying job to holding office, even representing your home town? All kinds of corruption are possible while the people remain inattentive.

Where are any representative's loyalties when lobbyists and other big shots are manipulating and influencing government officials in the US as well as around the world? Other than as a trough of money of gigantic proportions, how does such a person or a company of such persons view the government of the United States?

America's founders knew one thing: The republics of history all died when narrow interests overwhelmed the common good and the interests of the commonwealth. Not only must we pray that America is not bequeathed a similar fate, we the people must continue to smarten up and don't be chumps for the bad guys; pay attention at all times to the scoundrels at the top, remember not to trust them, and make sure you do what you need to do to place the bums with solid American citizens.

Chapter 2 Senator Gary Hart Makes a Lot of Sense.

Hart no longer sounds like a liberal, progressive Democrat.

On June 26, 2015, former US Senator Gary Hart, who gave up his Senate seat when he became the clear frontrunner for the Democratic nomination in the 1988 election, affirmed in a well-crafted 2015 essay that Senators are basically windbags and either are corrupt or are waiting for high bid to become corrupt. Hart turned 80 years old his last birthday but he still looks young enough to help us believe that 80 is the new 50.

Many recall that Hart never finished his second campaign because he enabled his own seduction by a 29-year old model and never recovered politically. From being at the top, Hart went down hard and quickly. Many have written about Hart's mistake so I do not plan to add anything about that.

I do believe in redemption, however, and despite what some might call a character flaw, there is a place for Gary Hart in America's recovery if he wants it. The mind of Gary Hart has a lot that it can do to help America clean up its act. I commend him for his recent work and specifically for the excellent essay that he wrote in 2015. I used some of the facts in this essay already in Chapter 1. There is a new Gary Hart for sure and I do hope we see more of him.

Here are some great paragraphs from his revealing piece:

"...Justice O'Connor took her story title from a belief of the French Jesuit philosopher Pierre Teilhard de Chardin. Teilhard de Chardin believed that all good would rise and that all that rose would eventually converge. We pray that he was right for, at the present moment, we have only prayer and no evidence. In the realm of twenty-first-century American politics, the opposite is surely coming true."

Hart continues: "Welcome to the Age of Vanity politics and campaigns-for-hire featuring candidates who repeat their sponsored messages like ice-cream-truck vendors passing through the neighborhood. If the current Supreme Court had been sitting during Watergate in 1974, it would not have voted 9–0 to require the president to turn over legally incriminating tapes but instead would have voted to support the use of illegal campaign contributions to finance criminal cover-ups as an exercise in "free speech."

"What would our founders make of this nightmare of corruption? We only know, in Thomas Jefferson's case, for example, that his distrust of central government had to do with the well-founded and prescient suspicion that its largesse would go to powerful and influential interests, especially financiers, who knew how to manipulate both the government and the financial markets. In particular, Jefferson envisioned sophisticated bankers speculating in public-debt issues with some if not all the interest incurred going into their pockets.

"He [Jefferson] was way ahead of his time. The limits of his imagination would not have encompassed the early twenty-first-century financial world where vast sums of money are manipulated like the world's greatest three-card-monte game and nothing tangible is being produced—except fees and more money. Even the titans ruling over this game confessed, after the 2008 financial collapse, that they did not know what collateralized debt obligations, bundled derivatives, and other tricky instruments devised by clever twenty-eight-year-olds were about. All they knew was how to respond to their industry lobbyists' requests for very large contributions to compliant members of congressional finance committees and to do so quickly and often. And they did get their money's worth.

"The scope and scale of this genuine scandal (as distinguished from vastly more mundane behavior that passes for scandal in the media) is the single greatest threat to our form of government. It is absolutely incompatible with the principles and ideals upon which America was founded. At the very least, we Americans cannot hold ourselves up to the world as the beacon of democracy so long as we permit, as long as we acquiesce in, corruption so far beyond the standards of the true republic that our government cannot be proclaimed an ideal for other aspiring nations.

"On a more personal level, how can public service be promoted as an ideal to young people when this sewer corrupts our Republic? At this point in early twenty-first-century America, the greatest service our nation's young people could provide is to lead an army of outraged young Americans armed with brooms on a crusade to sweep out the rascals and rid our capital of the money changers, rent seekers, revolving door dancers, and special interest deal makers and power brokers and send them back home to make an honest living, that is, if they still remember how to do so.

"What angers truly patriotic Americans is that this entire Augean stable is legal. Even worse, recent Supreme Court decisions placing corporations under the First Amendment protection of free speech for political purposes compounds the tragedy of American democracy. For all practical political purposes, the government of the United States is for sale to the highest bidder.

A harsh judgment? Indeed. But it is impossible to claim to love one's country and not be outraged at how corrupt it has become. For former senators and representatives to trade a title given them by the voters of their respective states and districts for cash is beyond shameful. It is outrageous."

Thank you, Gary Hart. Your words are solid and well needed today. Please keep writing. Get on the talk shows. Thank you again.

Thomas Jefferson is often quoted by patriotic writers, including Gary Hart. Our third president is under attack today by Antifa and others who claim a slave-owner who prayed to God and wanted to abolish slavery cannot be a good man. Yet, even Juan Williams, liberal columnist from Fox news suggests that Jefferson is one of the greatest patriots in American History and he is one of Williams' most favorites.

Jefferson wrote: "I tremble for my country when I contemplate that God is just." Those words of Thomas Jefferson, can be read on his memorial. They referred to the institution of slavery. Today he would readily provide the same judgment about corruption in and of the American Republic. He was one of the patriots, who wrote the Declaration of Independence and the Constitution so he would surely know. He would not approve of the knaves who seek office for their own aggrandizement and then they look at their terms of office as one day of huge grab bags after another.

Can you imagine if you were able to hear an address from George Washington, James Madison, Jefferson, John Adams, and the best writer of all the patriots, Alexander Hamilton if they were alive and if they were inclined to observe today's lobbyists and special interest brokers at work, especially former government officials, organizing fund-raising events and delivering bundles of checks. They would be appalled. Even more, they would be ashamed. They would wish they were able to have carved out a republic where it was not only difficult for an official to be corrupt; it would be almost impossible.

Gary Hart likens the lobbyists and special interests of today, who frequent the halls of Congress, to the money changers in the temple of democracy. Hart cautions Americans to not make an error in underestimating the grave sins of public officials against the public.

"It is an error of serious proportion to dismiss corruption in twenty-first-century American democracy on the grounds that this has all been going on from the beginning, that boys will be boys, that politicians are always on the take." Hart is clearly disgusted with the good ole boys who were once his peers in officialdom. Don't you just love his candor. "Past incidents of the violation of public ethics provide no argument for accepting the systemic and cancerous commercialization of modern American politics." It makes me think that Gary Hart is a conservative. Thank you again, Senator Hart.

Hart understands the factors with which the founders wrestled. They were good men. They admired things that we do not even talk about much anymore—such as virtue. When the founders discussed virtue, they looked way back to ancient Athens and the ideal of the republic. They would not settle for a democracy and insisted that our government be a republic. Our founders believed just as the scholars of ancient Greek and Rome believed—that a republic with leaders who lacked virtue would not long survive.

Has that not been the issue during the past eight years pre-Trump. Though the jury is out on our new president, the signs look good that even if his past life was not one huge clump of virtue, as he has surely had his faults, admittedly, President Trump sure seems to me to be OK with God. And, he surely seems like he wants to do the right thing for his country, his loving family, and himself.

Virtue is the big issue today. If a virtue robot could look into the hearts of the press and most members of Congress, they would be at risk if they chose to throw the first stone at President Trump.

Gary Hart bellows out from his heart: "Just because it is legal doesn't make it right." He thinks this should be carved above every congressional doorway, every cabinet department, and even the White House itself.

Our Grab bag representatives have never met an unmarked bag they did not like. Hart found a good Democrat from the past to contrast with the knaves sponging off the people today pretending to be representatives. He asks Americans to compare the life of this fine Democrat to the poor behavior of today's under-oath politicians:

"Contrast the fact that upon returning to Independence, Missouri, in 1953, Harry Truman refused to take even a pencil from the White House ("It didn't belong to me," he said, by way of explanation) with modern presidents whose political networks have graciously waited until they departed the White House to make them rich."

We, who pay attention can see the erosion of the integrity of our governing system, and the principles and ideals underlying it, and worse than we could imagine, most officials are not at all like Jefferson Smith, who as a pure and honest man, though a bumpkin, when off to Washington as a replacement Senator, believing the game was clean and fair. Smith found that even the Senator that he admired most, Senator Joseph Paine, was part of the corruption. It was everywhere and is everywhere today.

WC Fields would say: "Don't be afraid my little Chickadee, my little Moon Cow, not everything is as it seems." Gary Hart is out of the

Senate so he is no longer being pulled to do evil at the behest of the scum of the earth- those who Donald Trump rightly called the Swamp.

Hart believes that we must Restore the *Republic of Conscience.* He knows that requires a major reduction and eventual elimination of what he calls ***the integrity deficit***. When Hart talks about making things right again for America, he always includes virtue. The national interest, what is best for our country and coming generations, has no place on the back door of slimy offices. If the bad guys think they can be bad and nobody in America cares, we will see a lot of badness before anything gets good. If the bad guys are politicians, with power, we cannot afford a minute more of their "leadership."

Gary Hart, in the role of let's say the great evangelist, Billy Graham, says the question is: "By adhering to its highest principles and ideals, will America continue to have the moral authority to lead all people of goodwill?"

What choice do we have? We must have the courage as a people to drive the money changers from the temple of democracy and recapture government of the people, for the people, and by the people. Don't you like how that sounds?

In his essay, Gary Hart makes some conclusions that I affirm" "We are not the same country we started out to be. We cannot conduct our political process the way we are doing in the twenty-first century and claim to adhere to our earliest principles. We must decide who we are. And if that decision is to restore our highest ideals, then major changes must be made in the way we elect our presidents and our members of Congress. Amen, Senator Hart!

Much of this chapter and the prior one can be credited with the fine work by Senator Gary Hart, who until I read his piece from start to finish, was not on my most favored persons list.

Gary Hart is a former United States senator and presidential candidate and the author of 21 books. From THE REPUBLIC OF CONSCIENCE *by Gary Hart. Article was published by arrangement with Blue Rider Press, a member of Penguin Group USA. Copyright © 2015 by Gary Hart.*

Chapter 3 Americans Are Mad as Hell about Dwindling Rights!

Swinging lefty delivers no dreams

Hollywood from 2009 through 2016 was fairly solidly behind all Democratic leaders, both in Congress and in the White House. Now, in 2017, that there is no longer a Democrat on Pennsylvania Avenue, they are no longer behind the President at all. In fact, though he was once a TV star, they absolutely hate him. Of course, not every star feels that way. Hillary Clinton had far more celebrity supporters than Donald Trump, but his 37 celebrity fans turned out to be the ones who backed the winning candidate.

One might conclude that it does not matter in which neighborhood you live. As long as you swing with the lefties, you can be assured of love and respect from the Hollywood elite—even if they do not know you from Adam. FYI, Hollywood does not care about your rights or mine—just theirs!

By the way, it does not matter if you are a politician or a reprobate, or you happen to simply be a member of the low information crowd. If you vote on the left side of the ballot box with the communists, and the redistributionists, you are welcomed with open arms in the town with its name on the hill. Welcome to Hollywood!

Today Americans on the left and the right are being asked to give up their rights so that others, who are jealous of those rights, can be made happy. Today's government leaders in both parties lean left and love to call themselves progressives. Being a progressive today gives some American rights that the founders never dreamed anybody would need or want.

For example, a progressive has the right to lie up a storm and he or she has the right to expect the corrupt media to swear that their word is the Gospel. A progressive can always say they did not take the cookie from the jar, even if their finger prints are all over the jar, and Lieutenant Columbo is saying: "Oh, oh, one more thing, before I forget..."

The point is that liberal progressives seem to have more rights than reality can imagine—including the rights to lie, cheat, and steal with impunity, especially if the real victim is a conservative.

The media enjoys covering for any lefty that lies. The low information crowd (LIC) has lost the ability to discern a lie from the truth. Therefore, lies do not affect the likeability or the electability of a politician. By the way, LICs cannot even discern the meaning of the word discern. That's why our country is in trouble. LICs brag about their lack of knowledge on most subjects when interviewed on the Late-Night TV celebrity road trips. But their dumbness is not really funny.

We live in a world in which real scandals are mocked as fake scandals and late-night TV hosts are supposedly the only ones who can tell a real scandal from a "fake scandal."

Some of the scandals about which we have learned from government and media sources are in the fake variety according to official government sources.

For the longest time, a sure way to throw off the LICs so they would always lean left was to blame Bush for everything imaginable. Ironically, now with Trump as the President, even the Bushes are blaming the new President and they have given the left a pass.

I do not want to be disrespectful to the institution of the US Presidency. Yet, many of us recall that when cornered, President Obama often said that he got his news from the newspapers, not the White House Daily Briefing. Charles Krauthammer, a paraplegic who still has one of the sharpest mind on the planet, found this a bit problematic. These are his words:

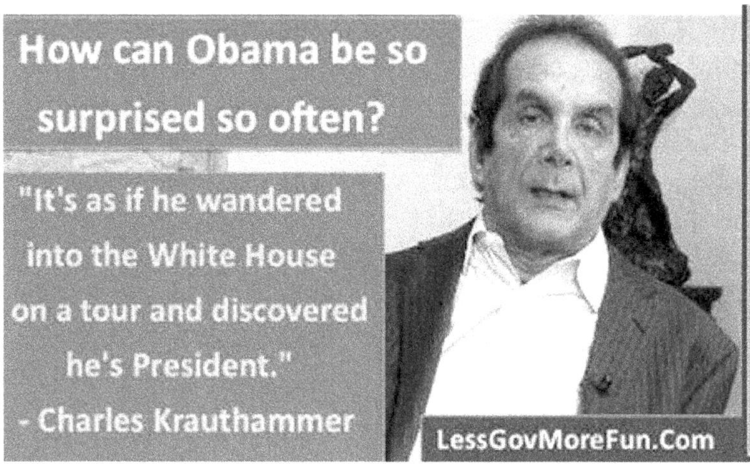

Every now and then, a Hollywood guy goes off the farm or as some say: "*off the reservation*," and insists on telling a new truth, which most often makes the old lies look like they too are true. It is a great trick and it can deliver a lot of laughs in Hollywood if delivered properly. Moreover, it can make the lefties seem smart at times.

Some elitists may say that only those Americans who are really stupid are unaware that the former president was really mad as hell that such things as what he called "the fake scandals" could actually happen. They also suggest that this president would get even "madder" when he had to read the newspaper to find out about the fake scandals as his advisors seemed to want to concentrate on real scandals. They "knew" he is working hard to make everything better—working really hard because he loves America deeply and his love of America is shared equally with, ahem, the First Lady. OK, maybe this paragraph was all fake.

Our country's former president, our one-time CEO, the leader of the free world, would have gladly served in Vietnam but was too young (just six years old) and at the time, unfortunately, he was also living in a Muslim Country (Indonesia), but not as a Muslim, though attending a Muslim school. Regardless of his tender age, they would not have released him for military duty anyway. I think.

At the time, being six years old was not the major reason for the former to not have been able to serve America in Vietnam. As an aside, the largest Muslim population in any country is in Indonesia, but of course that does not cast any aspersions upon anybody mentioned in this chapter.

The Leader of the free world before 2017, wanted all Americans to believe that he had the best intentions and regardless of the crisis du jour, or as the Republicans would call it, the "scandal du jour," he would use his patented formula, which he developed from his substantial personal experience in the free world. "He will study the situation and take the most appropriate action—but only when the time is right." Who could want for more?

Just as the leader of the Free World, our former president, I too am mad as hell about a government that permitted America to be demeaned by either incompetence or intentional efforts towards its destruction.

However, this is not the purpose of this book, though government lies do limit all of our rights that are enumerated in the Bill of Rights and the Constitution. It is however, the underlying truth about why I wrote the book. Would it not be nice if we all told the truth—especially if the truth tellers were high ranking government officials?

In case you missed it in one of my recent books, we're going to offer a scenario from a movie similarly in this book, but we will quickly get on to the meat of the US Bill of Rights, the precious adjunct to the most wonderful document other than the Bible itself—written by the hand of God. I speak of course of the US Constitution.

In essence, Americans are upset today because our Constitution is under attack, and the Constitution is the framework that enables our Bill of Rights. As most historians, and those who studied sixth grade history once knew, the Bill of Rights enumerates specific rights for Americans above and beyond the general rights for all US citizens, which are provided in the US Constitution.

The Constitution which is the big boss over the Bill of Rights says that any rights not so enumerated in the Constitution belong to the people, not the government. Think about that. It means that the government aka, a rogue president such as our past president could not legally countermand any piece of the Constitution, including any of its amendments. Of course, our past president did so anyway by operating illegally and the Congress did not challenge him.

Today's government officials as we all know, unfortunately seem to see it differently. By the time you finish this book, you will have no sympathy for them.

The Constitution—the law of the land—the basis for the Bill of Rights, which you are about to explore in depth, has unlawfully been surpassed by opportunists today in government. That makes a lot of US "Mad as Hell!"

Howard Beale in the paragraphs below represents all frustrated Americans. His story, though unrelated to the theme in the book, really captures the mood and the emotions of America today regarding a government gone wild! *Wild* in this case is a synonym for ***"bad."***

You may not remember because you are probably not old enough, but you will like this story regardless. Many of you do have enough life mileage to have seen the movie we now discuss long after its debut in 1976.

Back in November 1976 Howard Beale, as played by Peter Finch, the long-time anchor in the "Hollywood" movie "Network News," gets the bad news that eventually causes him to utter one of the most famous movie lines of all time.

Beale gets fired and is given two weeks. The long-time anchor has a very poor reaction to this news and he cannot control himself during the next news broadcast. You get the feeling that he saw his perceived "rights" being violated.

He feels he is penned in and cannot move forward. With a minimal amount of thought, he promises to commit suicide on the air. The company therefore, immediately fires him—no second chances for a repeat performance.

Beale is naturally devastated and remorseful. He begs for the opportunity to say good-by to his fans with dignity, and his producers think it might be good for the show so they give him his last opportunity ever for air time so that he can say his good-by's to his public and also apologize. He gets his chance

Peter Finch as Howard Beale in Network News

Yet, once on the air, the one-time network news anchorman is overwhelmed by his continuing circumstance. He goes into another diatribe starting off with a rant claiming that "Life is bullshit." He is so passionate that his ratings spike as he persuades his viewers to shout out of their windows: "I'm as mad as hell, and I'm not going to take this anymore!" That is the line heard 'round the world.

Well, my fellow Americans, I bet you saw this coming, and I am going to deliver it as passionately in words as I can: "Like you, I am mad as hell, and I am not going to take this anymore." I know you are too. No more corruption! Let me remind you. Besides one rights violation by government after another, there are the usual issues, but those issues are far worse today than ever before in our country's history. Now that we are mad as hell, we know what we must do.

We the people must continue to smarten up and never be chumps for corrupt politicians. Your job like mine is to keep reading great books about your rights. Stop trusting government and begin to pay attention at all times so we know what the scalawags at the top are up to. Finally, we need to do what we must to replace these the bums in office with solid American citizens.

Chapter 4 The Corrupt US Government Is a Train Wreck

Find something right about government

Taxes are too high, elected officials are out of touch, government is too big, spending is out of control, the Obamacare program has itself been a train wreck from its inception and Republicans in Congress do not care anymore. Obamacare has created fewer patients through neglect rather than by providing more cures. The VA system in Obama-times has been so bad that it looked like it might have been a secret plan to rid the government of the cost of too many patients.

Worse than anything else imaginable, heroes from Vietnam, Korea, Mideast Wars, and elsewhere, after killing the enemy and surviving—had begun to be killed one at a time by the VA System. Our past president ignored the problem. He never acted. Some would say these war survivors are dying in a VA system supposedly designed to keep them alive.

Nobody, after spending $160 billion per year supposedly on Veterans health care, would be able to explain why American heroes were ever neglected and continued to be neglected during the terms of the past president. Any Joe on the street could figure out how to provide for the health of veterans for $160 billion a year! Donald Trump is now the veteran's best friend and he is already making it all better. Moreover, the vets trust that our new president will get the job done.

Those people of America who choose to pay attention, see the federal government as incompetent. Moreover, the people today have known they have no voice. In Obama-times, we found our government exchanging five of the nastiest Taliban Officers at the top of their game, from Gitmo for one PFC who was a deserter. At the same time, a patriotic and heroic former Marine was rotting in a Mexican jail.

Sgt. Andrew Timorese was held at Tijuana's La Mesa Penitentiary. His release came after him rotting 224 days, which included a lengthy, closed trial and a Congressional hearing highly critical of Obama Administration efforts to secure his release and Mexico's refusal to let him go.

Can it be that "*too many of US are too lazy to hold government accountable, while too many of our finest are on the take.*" Are we getting the government we deserve or are we simply too trusting?

The past eight years of government created a big train wreck. Additionally, corporate leaches have found that it is pretty easy to infiltrate our government. They demand and take their take of the proceeds. We have record unemployment while illegal aliens are smiling as they take American jobs. Cunning kids are being advised how to enroll for US benefits at the border; an unsustainable status quo supports special interests over the people's interests—and when we look to the future we see a public education system that intentionally creates dummies with a *common core* that is rotten to the core, and intentionally so.

Today's high school graduates are so dumb that they don't seem to mind being called dummies. They expect whatever job they get to consist of drill and practice tests just like the *common core*, so they can do well.

What if instead of multiple choice, their jobs are more like essay questions requiring thought instead of rote memorization of answers to unasked questions? What if they are not simple True/False deals? Can the test oriented student of today succeed with just the common core? Scrooge would sum it up with a hearty "Bah Humbug." It is that bad and perhaps even worse!

Before President Trump took office, we had the poorest economy since the depression; excessive welfare and income redistribution; institutionalized lying; a corrupt state-loving press that carried water for government rather than voicing off for the people; a debt large enough to kill America; huge student debt stopping graduates' success; tyranny v. democracy; government lawlessness; freedom and liberty in jeopardy; American stagnation, and a big loss of America's world prestige. To make matters worse, we have a supposed free press, a supposed fourth estate, which is supposed to keep things from going south; but the press has gone south.

And, on top of that, for eight years, we had a top leader who claimed to have learned about what happened in his own administration from the daily paper. Yet this same supposedly competent person never chastised or fired his advisors whose missions were to keep him informed, apprised, and well-advised. Everybody who befriends the Democrats gets a free ride with no accountability. It is that bad. One could not be creating as much harm to America if they actually intended to do so.

Even as unbelieving as our past president presented himself, his word was accepted 100% by millennials, whose coffee-breath professors assured them that the past president was the real deal.

You may recall at graduation time in 2014, the administrators and the communist faculty and student lemmings at the State University of New Jersey, Rutgers, embarrassed Dr. Condoleezza Rice, a major US historical figure. They were nasty and unwelcoming and protested her choice as commencement speaker. Rice appropriately rescinded her acceptance. The president never offered a thought on the matter.

Their millennials idea of free speech continues to be that it is OK only if it is approved thought as determined by the Thought Police. Unfortunately, for Americans, more and more universities are carving out very small areas of their campus in which free speech may be practiced. In the past all of America, including all college campuses, every inch, were free speech zones.

The student loan burden prevents former student borrowers, trained by communist elite, from buying homes, cars, and having a family. The communist teachers think none of this is necessary anyway unless provided by the state.

We live in an age in which only retirees in their 90's seem to be able to afford the honeymoon cottages necessary to begin a family. As many as 40 million student loan borrowers are too broke to engage in basic life. College loans, instead of lifting people to the top, have created a new race to the bottom,

On the International stage, during the past eight years before Trump, America became a bad actor. Allies no longer could take US on our word. Israel, the continual voice of reason in the Mideast was being bullied by Vietnam Veteran John Kerry, then US Secretary of State, to capitulate to the many rockets from Hamas sent into their suburbs to kill innocent people. Kerry wanted to claim a diplomatic victory but cared nothing about assuring that the right team, a friend of America, won the engagement.

Would it not be better to not interfere with an Israeli victory and end the conflict once and for all? To what end did it serve the prior administration to be an obstacle to our great ally, Israel in its need to protect itself for the long haul. At the time, I wondered if the past president had read the papers to learn anything about Israel and its terrorist neighbors or he simply flipped coins or rolled the bones.

To make it worse, frustrated zealots from the left were making sure nobody gives America a break on the world stage. The leader of the free world for the last eight years was hell bent on making the rest of the world stronger by making America weaker. He highlighted perceived American weakness and then he apologized for America. His lack of honor for his own country did little to command respect for our country across the world.

Nobody in the world gave America standing ovations during the Obama years. Within Months of Trump's inauguration, even the Saudis were lauding President Trump in his fight against world terrorism. During the past eight years, terrorism could not even be mentioned as the word was banned. Nobody asked Obama's America for curtain calls. Our leaders had turned their backs on our friends and were paying homage to our enemies. How did anybody believe this was good for America?

Smaller and weaker countries such as Russia, Iran, and North Korea relentlessly pushed US around and laughed at US during the past eight years. Our only response was to see if somehow, we may have offended them—that somehow it was our fault. How many take-downs of Malaysian planes will it take for our enemies to resume taking US passenger planes out of the sky?

The new America for eight years, rather than rattling our enemies by promising and delivering quick doom for bad behavior, showed its greatness by counting the number of hits on a *hashtag of* ***bring our girls home,*** when no Americans were among those missing.

Our misinformed experts expected terrorists to cower when the number of twitter resends hit a million. We also refused to discuss why four Americans, including the Ambassador, were permitted to die in Benghazi when the military said that it was prepared to save them. We accept too many lies from our government. Perhaps none of us understand the major rights provided in the founding documents. It sure is time we learned and then acted to end this blatant corruption at the top.

We had an administration that was quick to blame anyone or anything but themselves. They had no problem blaming the Christian Government of Nigeria for not reaching out enough to the Muslim killers who kidnapped 300 girls as sex slaves. Boko Haram had captured and killed 49 boys just a few weeks before. The captors boldly announced they would sell the girls on the sex slave market, and the US appeared powerless in its feeble response. Unless you are a communist progressive liberal, you know this is wrong. Then, of course you would find real power in the empty hashtag!

Hundreds of thousands of illegal aliens have been invited to our country by President Obama in mid-2014 and long before in what some now call a humanitarian crisis. Others say it is the left's idea of removing the borders completely to encourage more poor and needy to come to America to increase the votes for big government and progressive policies.

Conservative military leaders suggest that it is dangerous for America as many terrorists and gang members are entering through the open borders while border guards are changing diapers.

I find myself asking the same questions as most sane Americans. What has happened to our good sense? Should there not be a set of laws written by sane people and enforced by people who have taken oaths to do so. Such insane acts should not be permitted to occur without retribution?

Why do our representatives and yesterday's president not represent America? Why does nobody pay attention to the Bill of Rights? Do we know our rights? Can knowledge of our rights help us in this upside-down world? I would not have written this book if I thought it could not.

For me, these were the worst days of America that I had ever witnessed. We have not yet recovered with our new president and our Congress is trying to turn back the hands of time to the prior eight years. They are obstructing our President at every decision point.

With the exception of the president, clear-thinking Americans look at today's national leaders from the swamp as buffoons, without the wherewithal to tie their own shoes. These leaders would like all Americans to be happy in a state of mediocrity, rather than having an opportunity to become outstanding. "Don't worry: Be Happy!"

If you have been paying attention, and I sure hope you have been as it is a civic duty, you know that there are even more issues than the exhaustive list we just walked you through. Isn't that a shame on US?

I think this is the reason that you bought this book. Thank you very much. As we speak, a dirty, incompetent, and corrupt Congress is trying to thwart the efforts of a president duly elected by the people from fulfilling his promises to the people. Who does Congress think it is? We must know our rights to survive in this strange world.

I like to repeat this. The Constitution is a survivor's guide to dealing with corrupt politicians. The *Bill of Rights* is an extra addition to assure that the people come first, and the government last.

We are on the right side and thankfully we are on the same side, and together we can all help arrest control of our leftist progressive government back from perpetrators wishing to destroy US. I would ask that we all give President Trump a shot at helping us. There are not many other billionaire's out there that think anything like the good people of America think.

We first must understand what is going on and we then must understand our rights. Even before you and me, and everybody else are on board, just like Howard Beale, we must start the first wave of solutions by opening our windows all the way and shouting as loud as we all can: "I am mad as hell, and I am not going to take this anymore."

Then, you and I must make sure that we talk to all of the other people out there who you and I know—people like you and I and others, and let's help them know that unless we all fully engage in America, when we wake up from our deep fog, there may be no America left for our progeny.

We will have blown it for sure if that is permitted to happen.

Stay mad as hell as I am and it will help us all.

Chapter 5 Paul Harvey's Advice to the Devil

Paul Harvey knew the problems years ago

Paul Harvey was on the people's side.

Many know the name *Paul Harvey* as one of the most famous radio personalities of the 20th century. He was on the air in 1964 when at 16 years of age, I heard him on the radio of the 1963 Chevy Impala, with two brake petals, that my safe driving instructor Ralph Evans used to help me become a safe driver.

Radio Legend Paul Harvey's last newscast was February 7, 2009. Three weeks later, he died on February 28, 2009, at the age of 90 at a hospital in Phoenix, Arizona, surrounded by family and friends.

The "most listened to man" in broadcasting passed away on this particular Saturday after more than seven decades on the air. He was a venerable radioman for sure. Paul Harvey's folksy speech and plain talk are only available today as rebroadcasts on no more. Harvey died at the age of 90 at a hospital near his winter home in Phoenix

Paul Harvey first went on the air in 1933, and with shows like The Rest of the Story he was a staple of America radio for decades.
He was also a devout Christian who was deeply concerned that the United States was abandoning God and morality at her own peril.

Paul Harvey could have written this book in far fewer words as he seems to have hit on most of what I say in this book in a timeless essay that was first published in 1964.

He expressed his sentiments about those who seem to have no problem giving up America by offering some free advice to Satan. In his most powerful words and voce he blew away an unbelieving world in 1964 with his classic radio essay "If I Were the Devil."

As noted, this essay first hit the airwaves in 1964, but it was revised slightly over the years to fit the times—not enough to take away its Nostradamus features. His essay warns against attacks on the credibility of the Bible, marriage, and family, and the promotion of pornography, socialism, and gambling, among other things. Like Gary Hart, Thomas Jefferson, and Billy Graham, Paul Harvey hated corruption wherever it existed.

He also believed correctly that the source of corruption was in most cases the Devil.

"In other words," he concludes at the end of his essay, "if I were the devil, I'd just keep right on doing what he's doing." His point is that American culture is already promoting these evil things. Corruption should be abhorred but even back then Harvey worried that it had become venerated.

His essay is prescient because many of the very things Harvey was worried about in the 1960s have gotten much worse, to the great detriment to souls and America.

Here is the transcript of a version of his essay that appeared in 1996:

> If I were the prince of darkness, I would want to engulf the whole world in darkness.
>
> I'd have a third of its real estate and four-fifths of its population, but I would not be happy until I had seized the ripest apple on the tree — thee.
>
> So, I would set about however necessary to take over the United States.
>
> I'd subvert the churches first, and I would begin with a campaign of whispers.
>
> With the wisdom of a serpent, I would whisper to you as I whispered to Eve: "Do as you please."
>
> To the young, I would whisper that the Bible is a myth. I would convince the children that man created God instead of the other way around. I'd confide that what's bad is good and what's good is square.
>
> And the old, I would teach to pray after me, "Our Father, which are in Washington ..."
>
> Then, I'd get organized, I'd educate authors in how to make lurid literature exciting so that anything else would appear dull and uninteresting.

I'd peddle narcotics to whom I could. I'd sell alcohol to ladies and gentlemen of distinction. I'd tranquilize the rest with pills.

If I were the devil, I'd soon have families at war with themselves, churches at war with themselves and nations at war with themselves until each, in its turn, was consumed.

And with promises of higher ratings, I'd have mesmerizing media fanning the flames.

If I were the devil, I would encourage schools to refine young intellect but neglect to discipline emotions. I'd tell teachers to let those students run wild. And before you knew it, you'd have drug-sniffing dogs and metal detectors at every schoolhouse door.

Within a decade, I'd have prisons overflowing and judges promoting pornography. Soon, I would evict God from the courthouse and the schoolhouse and them from the houses of Congress.

In his own churches, I would substitute psychology for religion and deify science. I'd lure priests and pastors into misusing boys and girls and church money.

If I were the devil, I'd take from those who have and give to those who wanted until I had killed the incentive of the ambitious.

What'll you bet I couldn't get whole states to promote gambling as the way to get rich?

I'd convince the young that marriage is old-fashioned, that swinging is more fun and that what you see on television is the way to be.

And thus, I could undress you in public and lure you into bed with diseases for which there are no cures.

In other words, if I were the devil, I'd just keep right on doing what he's doing.

Think about Thomas Jefferson. Think about the newly reconstituted ageless Gary Hart. Think about the great evangelism of Billy Graham exhorting all of us to do well by God and man. Now, think about Paul Harvey who was rich for sure because his talent was great but whose concern for mankind was lit up like a huge Christmas tree when he broke ranks with many in the media, simply because he loved God and hated the Devil, and he offered this essay for us all so we knew how bad things had become—bad enough for us to know if we let it continue, the Devil would win.

Paul Harvey was betting that if we knew who Satan actually was, we would reject him and that is the purpose of his essay. It fits perfectly in this book about rights and how to correct the corruption in our midst.

Chapter 6 The USA Is a Constitutional Republic!

A Representative Democracy

We have set the table well for this chapter. We now know that the United States is a suffering giant with caretakers who care more about their personal bank accounts than the people they represent.

None of us, even when we decide to act to save the nation, can do well in defending America without having facts at our disposal. Understanding the Constitution which grants every right to the people except for a few select rights to government such as building an army for defense and maintaining interstate highways, and regulating commerce between the states, and very few others, helps us know that we the people own America, not *it* the government.

My sister Nancy, a very bright person four grades ahead of me taught me the meaning of the word, redundant. We have a phenomenal Bill of Rights formed as the first ten changes to our Constitution, which provide things like freedom of speech, religion, and a bunch of other rights including the right to bear arms.

The irony here is that the explicit Bill of Rights are redundant as all the rights in the Bill of Rights are provided implicitly in the Constitution itself. How is this? Simply by granting the people all rights other than those explicitly granted to the government. The default is that such rights are denied to the government.

Nonetheless, extrinsically pronouncing these rights in the Bill of Rights made a lot of early Americans comfortable with the new government and today they make a lot of us comfortable that the government cannot pretend to have any of the rights deemed specifically for the people.

Other good stuff in the Constitution

The Constitution prescribes that the US is a representative democracy, which as you probably already know means that because we have an elected chief executive (president) and a constitution, it makes our country a *republic*. A republic is a better deal for all Americans than simply a democracy.

Most of us know the pledge of allegiance, which was once mandatory to recite daily in US schools at the beginning of the school day. However, at that time there was no question about whether our government believed that Americans should love America.

The "Pledge" contains the words: "...and to the *Republic* for which it stands." Our great, and wonderful and rightfully proud country is thus both a representative democracy and a republic.

When we think of the very important notion that "America is a representative democracy," watching the "clowns" from both parties, who occupy our central government, it is a sane question to ask if this is really true.

The song, "Is that all there is?" comes to my mind. We are nothing like our parents and nothing like our founders. We have reason to be ashamed of our corrupt government, but then again, our country today is so far off the founders' mark that even shame cannot squeeze in under the line as being politically correct.

Our representative democracy is the foundation of America. However, what makes America—America is that we are also a republic—the finest form of government ever brought forth from mankind. The Bill of Rights, the main curative subject for corruption in this book is just an add-on to an unending list of inalienable rights for the people—you and me.

The part that those not educated in civics, like the youth of our times and the know-it-all millennials, do not understand is that government has no rights under the constitution other than those specifically granted by the people. Government also has no money and no resources other than the taxes they steal from regular Americans.

Government is not the answer. If it were any kind of answer it would deliver poorly on your expectations. Government was set up to be the people's slave but there are people looking for gifts from its own slave labor given to the government. They have given the government far greater powers than the constitutional democracy (republic) permits.

Thus, when the government goes awry as today, it must be reined in. But, you already know that as you are one of the chosen to read this book about your rights as a citizen of the USA. Those who do not know this are prepared to permit this country to be ruled by the government for the government and let the people be damned!

America has a great set of laws, beginning with our Constitution, the primary law of the land. These laws govern all people and all politicians in perpetuity—as long as ***we*** choose to hold our politicians (aka elected officials) accountable.

The fact that we Americans no longer hold our officials accountable is why they are not accountable. It is our fault. We get the government we deserve as we look for favors from scummy, filthy, dirty politicians and scalawags, when in fact it is they who owe allegiance to us in our role of "we the people."

What is a republic?

To answer the first unasked question first, let me say "No!" You do not have to be a Republican to live in a republic. Forget about political party labels. The founders brought forth America and expressly forbade the inclusion of political parties in our government. Republican and Democrat are identifying terms to political parties that evolved over many years in America. They could just as easily be called Party 1 and Party 2 and their meaning would be the same.

Republicans have nothing to do with a republic and Democrats have nothing to do with a democracy. When we come to grips that the type of democracy that we have is for all the people from all parties and it is a constitutional democracy (having a constitution), that makes it a republic. That's that! A democracy with a constitution, a set of basic laws, is a republic, even if it consists of people, none of which are Republican. It is also a constitutional represented Democracy, even if it consists of people none of which are not Democrats.

The simple definition of a republic (from Latin -- res publica), is as follows: a state in which supreme power is held by the people and their elected representatives, and which has an elected or nominated president rather than a monarch.

That is us folks. As long as we believe that, we should also believe that neither the Congress nor a President no matter how loved by Democrats or Republicans can violate the Constitution by executing laws that have never been passed by the legislature. President Obama admitted this and then violated his very own words on multiple occasions. That is pure corruption.

In practice in a republic, the government is ruled by elected leaders run according to law. The law in our country is called **The Constitution**. Unlike a democracy, a republic is not based only on majority rule. The law of the land, a Constitution which contains a set of dos and don'ts gives the minority a voice.

Moreover, the majority cannot decide in such a government that Brian W. Kelly, your humble author, can be summarily executed since he does not measure up to the majority's expectations. The Constitution does not permit such vile action. In a republic, it takes lots more than that and that is why real laws are important to us all.

Our biggest and most important laws within the US Constitution are written so that the government cannot hurt US or impose its will upon US without our explicit consent. Our country was founded by some very smart people and they knew that without constraints on any government, which could potentially go wild, the people could not and thus, would not win.

The constraints in the Constitution are implicit in that all of the rights are owned by the people, and only those rights explicitly given to government are for the government. The only purpose of the Bill of Rights is so that Americans know where their starter set of rights begin. Government has no additional rights.

Let me repeat. Government has no rights other than those granted by law to the government by the people. The people have all the rights. A government that subjugates the people for its purposes is expressly forbidden in these United States of America.

This great body of law known as the Constitution therefore makes politicians and others in government fear a backlash when they attempt to deny the people, even just one person, our liberty and freedom. In a pure democracy, if the majority decided that you or I should be killed, nothing would necessarily stop it if it were to be. But, in a republic such as ours, it is the rule of law which prevails and the rule of law starts with the Constitution. Many of our elected officials at all levels of government today do not understand the minimal authority of the government. Nobody and no government can determine that a person can be killed unless it has been a determination of the courts. Majorities can kill nobody.

It seems for sure that many in our nation today, mostly on the far left, are trying really hard to kill America's America by demeaning the Constitution and the Bill of Rights in particular. With majority rule in a pure democracy, the only problem is that you may not be in the majority. Then what?

You more than likely selected this book to help fight off those who do not respect our fundamental laws. If the courts stay honest, and that is not assured, the people will always prevail because the laws are on our side.

If you could figure any way to put an unmovable grip on corrupt politicians, right now or in the future, would you not do so? The founders of America put such a stranglehold on all political agents of the future when they wrote and adopted the US Constitution, the greatest body of law ever written in any civilization. Government has no inalienable rights. Such rights are reserved for the people, and many of those rights are explicitly listed in the Bill of Rights!

The problem of course is that government administers public things such as cities, states, and federal agencies as well as the "public" schools. But, the people are the masters of government at all levels as well as the public schools. This matters not one iota if the people do not understand they are the masters and not the slaves. If officials do not follow the law, the people must step in to stop the perpetration.

However, if we the people do not know what is written in the Constitution, or the Bill of Rights, it cannot help America too much. Can it? So, it is time for all Americans who have not been paying attention to stop being dummies, political sport (chumps) for the elite. It is time to rule America as our birthright as citizens of this great country commands US to do. Let somebody else eat cake!

And, so, my fellow Americans, that is the number one reason that in order to form a more perfect union of the original thirteen colonies / states, and with more states expected after the first thirteen, our forefathers built the finest Constitution ever fashioned by a pen in human hands.

The Bible, from the hand of God, may be the greatest story ever told in the greatest book ever written, but the Constitution is as good as it gets for the goodness of man, written by the hands of our first patriots. Surely, this document was written with the guidance of God.

In this day and age, there are everyday attempts by the government, which is controlled by the far left on the ideology spectrum, to undermine our lasting republic, which is an almost pure constitutional representative democracy. As noted, the attacks most often come from the left side of the political spectrum, which is the side that would in a heartbeat would replace our Constitution with books written by Marx and Engels.

Democracy is the opposite of communism

You would doubt me only if you knew nothing of our founding and the anti-people notions of Marx and Engels. The ideology of the progressive left today, masquerading as the Democrat Party, along with the corrupt press favor Marxism in its simpler forms of socialism and communism.

Since Americans do not as a rule vote for socialists, communists, or Marxists, these are things that nobody other than a crooked politician would want. Even though far left politicians desire these ends, they will not openly speak about the socialist or communistic state which they espouse because they have not duped the people enough. So, to a large extent the people would resist but the persistent left is wearing many Americans down.

If you are unaware of this in today's government, I would recommend that you consider paying more attention. No politician wanting to be elected will admit that they are more communist than American. Yet, as much as it pains me to tell you, unfortunately, they are!

The overtures, which demean the Constitution, the fabric of our democracy, originate from corrupt politicians who have been caught up in the leftist movement, which would like to end capitalism, and bring on a socialist / communist order in which they were the leaders. They want to replace the American Dream, and all the dreams of *We the People*! And they would love it to happen so they could be our leaders in a communist world without having to fire a shot.

The people have the responsibility of keeping government honest!

Most of the time in our great form of government, we can sit back and let other good people govern for us. What happens if they begin to govern for their own selfish interests? The founders thought this might happen They did not suggest that Americans sit on the couch and let this happen. They fought a revolution against old England so America would continue to be free and ruled by the people.

They founded a country in which it was up to all the people to understand our laws—first the Constitution, of which the Bill of Rights is key, and then to pay attention so that our leaders follow those laws. After having fought a revolution for freedom, the early Americans were not about to let those who opposed their desire for freedom to retake America and force another war of independence.

When today, our supposed dedicated leaders do not follow the laws of the land, we must learn to send them home every two, four, or six years, as determined by the term lengths as set forth in Constitution for our House (2 years), the President (4 years), and the Senate (6 years) respectively. Corrupt representatives do not deserve a second chance.

To say it more clearly: We get to throw the bums out and replace them with people of character on a regular basis. Don't give up; vote them out!

With the people in control our government has been able to work well for over 240 years. When we get bad apples, we must throw them away by voting them out. Of course, that means we must always vote in order for our choices to matter.

Representatives are to be of the people?

Though representatives are supposed to come from the people, a type of political class of elites has come about and seldom do we get to vote for representatives anymore—who are truly of the people. Groups of politicians and special interests in the same party group together to determine who gets their money and who will ultimately get the nomination. John Doe might as well not take a shot unless a lot of other John Doe's provide big help.

By understanding America better, and especially by understanding our Constitution and its built-in Bill of Rights, Americans have a far better chance of bringing good and honest government back to the people.

The way it now currently works, there is far too much separation between US, the electors, and them, the elected officials. Most officials choose to live in gated communities, unaware of what is happening on our streets in our communities with regular joes.

The Constitution provides that our elected officials are given the task to coordinate our pooled resources for the intended benefit of "everyone." Everyone is this country until recently meant all US citizens. But everyone is often not included? We see politicians taking credit for spending treasury dollars on things that simply buy themselves votes. Nobody wants this and so it is up to all of US—we the people—to change it.

Like Gary Hart said so well, our government is wholly unaccountable to w*e the people t*oday. The government rejects the fundamental principles of our founding and has no real legitimacy the further it drifts from the precepts of the Constitution.

The US was not designed for a government of the government by the government and for the government. The Constitution is the blueprint for our country's design. It was designed by a group of founding artisans to not only represent their artistic touch, but to be held as the behavioral creed of the people, for the people, and by the people, forever. What thinking human being blessed to be part of America, could ask for anything more?

If you think that life, freedom, liberty, property, and the ability to pursue your own happiness are simple notions, and *givens* in any civilization, get out your thinking cap, and think again. Why do people from all over the world crash our gates just to get in? The US is an exceptional country.

As a point of note, Rush Limbaugh, who is a great patriot, has a great explanation of American exceptionalism. "American exceptionalism is about the exception to the rule or the exception to the norm, not that we're better people, not that we have better DNA, not that we're smarter. We've had more freedom. We've had more liberty. Obama doesn't understand that."

Americans are exceptional in that we have full freedom and liberty in our country, and with that we can exceed all limits of ordinary expectation. Go to any other country, and this exception no longer applies.

Throughout our short history, the USA has been the freest nation in the world with rights withheld from government and rights given to the people by our Constitution and given specifically by the Bill of Rights.

Today as our country's foundation is being threatened from within, more than likely you are reading about the Bill of Rights and the Constitution so that you can extrapolate your American rights from this mélange of patriotic writings. When you finally get it and you understand your rights, you will then guard and protect your rights as well as work hard to protect this great nation, which provides them. It really is that simple.

If you had to give some rights up—which of your rights would you first give up? Your freedom? Your life? Your liberty? Your family? Your property? Or would you give up your ability to do what you needed to do to be happy? The sanest answer of course is "none of the above."

Who could ask for anything more than being an American? Ask the last arriving immigrant why they come here! We are free! But, if Americans do not care about our founding precepts to protect them from scoundrels, maybe our freedom, our lives, our liberty, our families, and our ability to do what we need to be happy, will be taken from us one day—perhaps in the not-too-distant future Maybe most of our rights lost over the last eight years, are already gone.

If the design of our nation, America, which the founders labored to create is so great, you might ask, why is it that our current lawmakers ignore it? Why are they so nefarious? Elected lawmakers have no trouble going with the flow and committing US to years of debt without even taking the time to read the debt-ridden legislation for which they vote. Neither the Constitution nor the Bill of Rights founders permitted today's Americans to bill future generations for the bills due today. Likewise, our public officials have no such rights. Our founders would not approve of what our representatives, including our past President for eight years, have done to our country.

Even worse, members of Congress, our alleged civil servants, the supposed representatives of the people, without even sweating, can get away without doing their jobs. At the same time, they are collecting more and more remuneration for their main act of either dallying or passing legislation for special interests, thus hurting the American people at large.

The true answer to that question [Why is it that our current lawmakers ignore the laws of the nation?] is very unfortunate for Americans. There is tacit collaboration in undermining the principles of our Democratic Republic by our supposed representatives, their supporters, the press, the special interests, lobbyists, and their corporate interests.

We the people now come last. They think we are not paying attention. Maybe we have not been paying enough attention but don't you agree that—that is about to end. *Pay attention* is about to become the motto of the free in America! Let the subjugated wish for more government! Let the free actively seek to keep our freedom and liberty!

Amen!

Chapter 7 A Country Populated by Immigrants

Legitimate immigration was necessary

Americans are all pro-immigration to the extent of our laws. If Americans were not pro-immigration for example, Columbus and his shipmates and their families more than likely would have withered away from disease or cold winters or they would have lost their battles with the Indians. Additionally, all fifty states; at least the mainland's forty-eight, would probably now have Indian derivative names, such as *Redskins*, and they would probably be run by the same financial wizards who run today's highly successful casinos.

After the USA was in operation as a country with a Constitution for just several years, its population was not much more than 4 or 5 million people. This is just a million or two more people than the annual flow of illegal immigrants from south of the border. This was of course before the illegal children revolution brought to us in our time by our immediate past president and his unconstitutional DREAM executive orders, because Congress did not give him his way.

Senator John McCain is a self-recognized expert on illegal immigration, having authored several bills that attempted to force amnesty in the name of comprehensive immigration reform down the throats of American citizens. In a letter dated February 2004, Senator McCain, recognized by many as a valid authority on the subject, noted that the flow of legal immigrants per years is in the millions and that the flow of illegal aliens, using 2002 as his year of reference is four million per year.

McCain stated emphatically in his letter that Border Patrol apprehension figures demonstrated that "almost four million people crossed our borders illegally 2002.Experts on the subject agree that illegal crossings have only increased since then until 2017 when under President Trump's watch, they are down to 30% of the norm.

If we were to add up the numbers from 1986 with President Reagan's amnesty and move forward from say 1991 when the effects of Reagan's amnesty would be fully realized, and if we use the lower figure of 4 million per year for 27 years through 2017, the total in our country illegally today would be 27 X 4 = 108 million. Personally, I think it is more like 60 million but either way, that is a lot of dependents for American taxpayers to carry.

History has recorded that on March 26, 1790, almost 225 years ago, the second session of the first Congress (operating under the Constitution with a real House and a real Senate) approved the new nation's initial effort to create the rules under which foreign-born persons could become U.S. citizens.

After these laws, from this point on, our borders were not open per se, and we had these laws (rules) for how those wishing to be Americans could come to visit or to become Americans. All Americans after this date, who immigrated were to follow the law of the land. The law put together in 1790 did not suggest as President Obama seemed to believe, that foreign interlopers go ahead and violate the US law, step on US soil, and then not worry about hiding from US officials because nobody would bug them.

The Naturalization Act of 1790 was specific in what needed to happen for foreigners to become citizens. The law specified that "any alien, being a free white person," could apply for citizenship, so long as he or she lived in the United States for at least two years, and in the state where the application was filed for at least a year. The new law also provided that "children of citizens of the United States that may be born ... out of the limits of the United States shall be considered as natural born citizens."

In effect, this law left out indentured servants, slaves, and women. It also mandated that one must "absolutely and entirely renounce and abjure all allegiance and fidelity to every foreign Prince, Potentate, State or Sovereignty." Though these terms were seen as quite generous, still the law denied the right to naturalize to "persons whose fathers have never been resident in the United States." Fair or not, this was the law of the US! It is not up to government employees, even if elected, to write their own laws.

Immigration law was becoming more important and the laws were changed several times since 1790. For example, in 1795, as anti-immigrant feeling began to grow in the country the Congress responded to the people's concerns. The necessary period of residence to become a citizen was increased from two to five years. Immigration law became firmer as the nation aged. Americans wanted America to be America, not a suburb of a country that wanted to be independent of America's laws.

Enter special interests, who like to bypass laws and have their friendly "owned" politicians let them get away with it.

Regarding immigration, you already know that there are two major special interests. The first special interest is the Democratic Party, which believes that if all illegal foreign nationals were to be immediately made citizens, the Democrat Party would never lose another election. That is a great motivator to bring all foreigners in immediately and make them all citizens of this nation. The corrupt press has aligned itself with the causes of the Democratic Party.

And, so, even though illegal alien workers have taken American jobs and driven down the average weekly wage, still your "friendly" Democratic Representatives in Congress advocate amnesty and citizenship for them, even if they break our laws. Your Congress promised less prosperity for all American citizens to accommodate foreign nationals that will help Democratic politicians continually get elected.

Unfortunately, most Americans, have yet to sign up for the theory that most of their representatives have become socialists and communists who are looking for a poor and continually underserved underclass, will vote these dishonest knaves back into office at their own peril.

The major concern of corrupt politicians is that the Democrat members of Congress get reelected and another Democrat president is elected next time and every time. One can explain the fanaticism of the left regarding President Trump. They simply cannot handle that their marked deck was discovered and their candidate was rejected.

Nonetheless, that really is the most important concern of the Democratic Party and it is also a major concern of the Republican Party. In other words, American citizens do not even register on our representatives' radar.

Bringing in poor, uneducated, people from south of the border, often criminals, who feed from our welfare system, taking tax dollars from those with minimal incomes, assures the Democratic politicians of the illegal's votes for a long time once they are in America. Who pays for these illegal aliens -- the working slobs such as you and I who happen to pay taxes or the poor bugger who was making $19.00 an hour in a meatpacking job and now there is no union at all, and they can work for $8.00 per hour if they do not complain. Illegal foreign nationals are tickled to get the $8.00. Plus, with multiple ID's the illegal foreign national can also collect unemployment and welfare and hold a job.

The second special interest is also against the people. They do not gain at the ballot box. However, illegal foreign nationals do provide huge gains in the wallets of American business. American businesses love paying the smallest wage possible and since illegal foreign nationals work for peanuts, there is a perfect marriage of needs. The point is both the leaders of the Democratic Party and the leaders of the Republican Party are fighting against American citizens (the voters) when they permit illegal aliens to live in America with impunity at the expense of American labor.

Traditional Republicans have great alliances with businesses. They are directed by their Republican donors, representing big businesses and corporations, to ignore the pleas of constituents who are out of work. Their job in order to continue the flow of donations to their campaign chests, is to assure businesses a steady flow of illegal cheap labor.

For their work in tamping down and delegitimatizing American sentiment about illegal aliens; is that they get big campaign contributions. The only groups, who align with the majority of Americans and who oppose blanket amnesty and who are 100% pro-American citizen philosophically, are conservatives, nationalists and populists, such as those who once were members of ad-hoc TEA Parties.

If you get a wrenching feeling in your stomach when you read TEA Party, I can explain it for you. The press today is corrupt, period. They are also very corrupting. They make you think that lies are truths and that truths are lies. They want you to hate all things conservative and all things Trump and all things TEA Party. They are joined at the hip with the progressive liberal Democratic Party, and do not support the people per se.

The corrupt US media has de-sensitized many Americans to their bias. The US media in many ways is anti-American but they do not tell you that they are communists. They do not want you to know.

They do not tell you that they do not give a damn whether you or your children do well in America.

Why? Well, they still want you to listen to them on the radio and TV and they want you to buy their newspapers and believe the slop they write. They know that if they tell you the truth, you won't like them much anymore.

So that you won't get to think it through by yourself, the media lied about the TEA Party right from the start. And, they lie about anything that hurts their progressive / socialist agenda and their backing of the Democratic Party. They do not deliver the real news to Americans yet most of US forgive them for their lack of honesty anyway. Americans love to forgive people—even those laughing at them as they stick a sword in their heart. Since they all have big popular names, they think the small people like US will take their "bull" and believe it. That was then and folks, this is now.

And, enough did as prescribed in 2008 and again in 2012 to elect and reelect the first bona fide incompetent president. Yes, he is known as the first black president though he is half black and half white. I believe that his white side is incompetent and his black side is fully competent, from my readings about his life. And, so, this is not a racist notion or an accusation. It is just an opinion based on facts as I see them.

Unfortunately for America, former president Obama and his brood in the deep state have not chosen yet to vacate fully their offices or virtual offices in the US government. After eight years, this residue still stains the offices of government workers in Washington and elsewhere.

As I read my facts in newspapers as did the former president, these sycophants of the former president, aka *the deep state*, are trying to tell us all that the new president is illegitimate. How do they know? Perhaps it is because he is not the old president but facts are used sparingly in their arguments. All I know is that this new guy in the Oval Office is the next best thing to Ronald Reagan and before that, it would be Jack Kennedy, another of my favorites.

If you are a hard and fast left-winger, the actions of the press may please you but if you simply love America, their actions should enrage you. We all need to know our rights to fight a dishonest press. Knowing that most of our rights stem from the Bill of Rights and the others directly from the Constitution means that we need to understand the contents of these bastions of freedom and liberty so that neither the deep state, nor other corrupt parts of government can have their way with US.

Conservatives differ on immigration with elitist Republicans, and opportunist Democrats. No American citizen, suffering from the worst economy since the depression would be asking the government to invite in more wage lowering workers. How does adding to the worker pool help American citizens get jobs?

Thomas J. Donahue, President of the US Chamber of Congress (C of C) told Republican Presidential Candidates (many current lawmakers) when deciding what issues, they would be for or against that "if they do not pass amnesty, the Republicans shouldn't bother to run a candidate in 2016."

The C of C represents the big donors who supported all the bad guys who Trump referred to as *The Swamp*. Why Trump's leanings against corrupt money changers does not soften his detractors does puzzle me. But, let's move on. The C of C cares nothing about workers' salaries but it cares a lot about corporate profits. Donohue, who is not a favorite of regular Americans, expected lawmakers to pass a John McCain, Lyndsey Graham, Jeff Flake and Marco Rubio style amnesty (Gang of Eight) amnesty bill rather than forego campaign funding from the Chamber.

Our most noteworthy Republicans, John McCain, Jeff Flake, Lyndsey Graham, sold out Americans for foreigners in this Senate-passed almost-law. Thank God, we have a House of Representatives that face the people every two years in real elections or the anti-American immigration stuff that these four Republicans tried to throw at us in 2014 might have stuck.

The US Senate, long controlled by Democrats, passed a global amnesty bill in early 2014. The goal was to nail Americans by giving their jobs to foreigners. Democrats do not like American citizens in need, who do not want to accept government help.

The Democrats, of which I admit I am one, have been pressuring the House of Representatives to do the same throughout 2014. The bill went down to a big defeat and our new President promises that all of the even breaks from now on will go to American citizens not illegal foreign national interlopers.

In Obama-times, the conservatives in the House blocked a vote on the McCain amnesty package, though Speaker Boehner, who must live in an all-white neighborhood, before he stepped down under pressure from regular people, appeared always ready to cave to the more powerful Obama and the Republican elite and the big ambidextrous donors in the C of C. This vote did take place and McCain, Flake, Graham, and Rubio lost but America won. Just this one time.

As a Democrat with little allegiance to the D party platform, I think I scribe honestly about what I see. I do see the Democrats at least as being honest about wanting to kill America. That is surely one of the D objectives. They do not deny it so how can we fault them for their bravery and honesty.

The Republican House was ambivalent at first in the McCain amnesty bill but then it defeated the bill that McCain et al had pushed through the Senate. If this had become law, the people would have had no choice but to throw out both houses of Congress and start over. The people have lots of power when we "pay attention."

By the way, I do have a solution that to 60,000,000 interlopers living in America while American costs are way too high to support them. The last book I wrote about the subject was called The Annual Guest Plan. In the next several weeks or months, I will be revising it to make it easier to understand without as many words.

We all want the immigration issue solved but not with the illegal foreign nationals owning our homes and forcing us to pay them for living here. My solution in this book and the next will tell Washington how to have a pro-American solution to the problem of 60 million illegal residents in our country who are not willing to leave without a deal. We actually have a pro-American deal.

The immigration issue is being put forth in this book to demonstrate that our legislators care more about other factors such as reelection and donations than they do about the people. Past president Obama, who theoretically could not run again, used Hillary Clinton as a surrogate to keep his legacy alive for four more years. Donald Trump spoiled their victory party and was hoping to wall-off America from perpetrators ready to overwhelm our country.

Obama, while having no terms left, participated in 400 fund raisers since his first election. President Bush for example went to about 200 at the same time in his presidency. Nobody thought that they had elected a campaigner in chief but that is what we got. The good news is that when the past president was campaigning, he was not working to destroy America.

We have more than enough illegal immigrants causing citizens to be out of work in the country right now. Otherwise, our real unemployment picture would not look so bad. Why would a party that hates the very notion of slavery bring more "slave labor" into the country when we know it will make the problem of making ends meet for American families even worse?

Perhaps too many of US, until things got this bad, had been hoping George would do it! Well, George Washington, one of our finest patriots is long gone, and unless you know of a recent George with the time, it is up to US to do it. Washington and Bush are gone.

Those in Congress who bow to special interests and their big donor base in the swamp should be made to take their final bows.

And, by the way, the two George Bush's did not get it done either. Now, they are acting as wounded babies and are saying that our legally elected president, Donald Trump is not a good guy. They add that he gets nothing done so they can make the Bushes look great and this sets the people up to get hosed by the Bushes again. Our past president and his two attorney generals did not try to give American citizens a fair shake. They were on the other team against American citizens. They chose not to enforce any immigration laws. Many Americans noticed that W did not do much better on this issue.

The Bushes did not follow the law of the land, the Constitution. They paid minimal lip service to the Bill of Rights except for the Second Amendment, which, like Obama, got a big X as neither Bush thought it should exist. This was tyranny for sure but with a divided Congress, it was tough to get action on behalf of the people. Now, with too many anti-Trumpers for America's good in the Congress and the Senate, and with the Bushes siding against America, it is like Obama is back in office again in the impregnable deep state.

This book is not about immigration. I have written enough immigration books. However, this book is undeniably about the Constitution and more specifically, the Bill of Rights. Both of these documents help all Americans to know that the laws are made for Americans to benefit. To demonstrate the lawlessness of the past administration and the disdain they have even for war heroes, here are a few anecdotes. Enjoy, and pay heed!

Without a scintilla of Constitutional authority, in the waning moments of his presidency, yesterday's president ordered well over 30,000 imprisoned criminals in illegal immigration status to simply be released so "they could be reunited with their families in the US."

Among them were rapists and murderers. The homicide and rape victims got no say. The criminals were released from prison into the US—not deported.

They got to go back on the streets of the US. Some Americans, thinking this was not a good deal for John Q. Public asked: "Did we really need 30,000 more criminals on our streets?"

Our immediate past president thought we should cajole and love the more than 60,000,000 souls in our illegal population, and he acted as if our laws did not apply to him or to the foreign nationals for which he advocated.

Meanwhile more than 30,000 American citizens in prison were not released concurrently so they could be with their families simply because they were not illegal aliens. I agree that American criminals should not be released but neither should foreign national criminals.

There is another true story that shows how ridiculous it is for the US to bend over backwards to coddle 30,000 criminals with illegal foreign national status. You may know that Mexican authorities punish Americans in Mexico for the smallest of infractions and will not free them even when there is national outrage in the USA.

For example, I already told you the story in this book that Mexican authorities held Sergeant Andrew Tahmooressi, a Marine war hero from Florida. He stood trial but to no avail. A Mexican judge in July 2014 sent him back to prison awaiting another appearance in August.

US outrage was expressed in a headline from Memorial Day Weekend, 2014: "Leave no man behind: Why is Team Obama unable to bring home Marine held in Mexico?" How inept a leader is a president who would like us to think he owns Mexico, yet he will not lift a finger to help a US Marine or go to the US border to see the immigration crisis of children first hand. Later many were wondering how today's President could free a deserter from the Taliban and completely ignore the plight of this hero Marine.

While on the battlefield, this brave Marine saved eight fellow Marines from the Taliban, and in a separate incident he saved a Marine from bleeding to death after he stepped on an IED and lost his legs. Tahmooressi also suffered a concussion when his vehicle hit an IED.

On March 20, 2014, the U.S. Department of Veterans Affairs diagnosed this young soldier with Post-Traumatic Stress Disorder (PTSD). Yet, even our past president would not lift a finger to get him freed from a Mexican Jail. Maybe the president did not expeditiously make the call, or maybe he simply did not like Marines? Or maybe he has no power? Maybe he does not like dealing with the Mexican government? Who really knows?

This unlucky former Marine simply mis-navigated the San Diego highways and ended up in Mexico. Rather than being treated with respect and returned, this hero Marine was apprehended and incarcerated and more than three months later, he was still there fearing for his life in a dreadful and very dangerous Mexican prison.

After a night in which he avoided death from a prison "Hit Squad," he was placed in solitary confinement with his four limbs chained to a bed. We treat no illegal foreign nationals with such cruelty. Maybe Mexico is trying to teach the US how to treat border violators?

Some of our rights spawned by the Constitution come about because the legislative branch (Congress,) formed by the Constitution creates additional laws. For example, no American can be captured and held by a foreign government unjustly. Here is how this law reads.

U.S. Code, Title 22, Chapter 23, Section 1732. It is entitled, "Release of citizens imprisoned by foreign governments."

Whenever it is made known to the President that any citizen of the United States has been unjustly deprived of his liberty by or under the authority of any foreign government, it shall be the duty of the President forthwith to demand of that government the reasons of such imprisonment; and if it appears to be wrongful and in violation of the rights of American citizenship, the President shall forthwith demand the release of such citizen, and if the release so demanded is unreasonably delayed or refused, the President shall use such means, not amounting to acts of war and not otherwise prohibited by law, as he may think necessary and proper to obtain or effectuate the release; and all the facts and proceedings relative thereto shall as soon as practicable be communicated by the President to Congress.

There is no excuse that Americans should accept for the president to not have gotten this Marine released. While this was ongoing, many Americans hoped and prayed that perhaps the past president, who sometimes learned about what was happening in the country by reading the daily newspaper, rather than being the Chief Executive and Commander in Chief, will use his old Sergeant Schultz standby excuse. Perhaps he has not been reading the papers and thus he has an out in not upholding another of our laws simply by saying as he does all too often. "I know nothing. Nobody told me." What a shame! Congress must force the President's hand to do his job.

Can it be that too many of US and too many of our friends have been Bill of Rights and other privileges "dummies" for too long? Perhaps understanding our rights and government limitations from the Bill of Rights and the Constitution, as well as your exhortations to all your friends will help many Americans awaken to what happens in a country in which government, rather than the people, has the stronger hand. Remember when government officials do not follow the people's commands, we get to un-elect them or impeach them. I'd say it is our play now!

This story has an end as given in a prior chapter. Somehow, when it looked like either Hillary Clinton or Donald Trump would be soon taking over the presidency, magically, the good sergeant was released from jail in the custody of his parents. Bravo for good true story endings!

Chapter 8 Remove Corrupt Politicians from America

Americans are way too trustworthy?

Our representatives are in office far too long and they gain relationships with other politicians who make up the ruling class. Instead of thinking about the folks in Danbury or Wilkes-Barre, or Clarks-Summit, or Santa Rosa, or Chicago, or Estero, Avoca, or Great Plains, or Orlando, our esteemed politicians begin to think they belong in Washington DC all the time, not in their home territories.

The social life in DC is lots better than most home towns, and our devoted representatives get to rub elbows with the hoity-toity, and the progressive Marxist communists that do not exist in their home areas. The facts are clear. They get corrupted.

All of a sudden, they are important, and being from Podunk or Plymouth does not matter. They begin to like the trappings of Washington more than being with their loved ones back in their home states. Though they insist on being called "the honorable so and so from such and such," few are honorable at all.

And they try to please the lobbyists and the special interests and the communists and others on their other team. They want to be liked and they want something in return that they don't get from the home town folks. Sometimes it is gifts; sometimes it is invitations to the best parties; and sometimes it is the promise of a great job if not reelected. The longer they are in Congress or in politics per se, the greater the opportunity for their personal corruption. They soil too quickly.

Unfortunately for all Americans, the new "important" relationships trump the notion of fair representation for the people (US) from back home. When they take their oaths of office and they promise to represent US, most are sincere at the time. That may be the last time.

Once they come to Washington, they experience the trappings and the temptations. And, because humans are only human, way too many of our finest stray from the mark and contribute to the re-creation of a country of which few thinking Americans are as proud today.

Americans share the blame

Yet, we Americans in many ways are to blame. We are either too kind or not enough self-assured that we trust them even after innumerable lies and self-aggrandizements. We can't believe they would do "that," yet they do. So, like lemmings, we go ahead and we call them hizzoner or herronner and worst of all, we re-elect them without thinking it through, because we think they really cannot be as bad as they are. Yet, they are as bad and even worse.

Yes, ladies and gentlemen, they are that bad. Please stop electing them. Their biggest fear is that someday all Americans will catch on by understand the Constitution chapter and verse. On that day, we will have all the rights, and they will have zero.

Think about our forefathers, especially George Washington, who guided our troops in the revolution against England's tyranny. Think about honest Abe Lincoln, who freed the slaves and saved the union. They would weep to see what their political successors, our representatives, have done to our nation. They will weep also because we let them get away with it.

So, our fair-haired representatives (figure of speech) choose to represent themselves and their special interests, rather than the areas of the country that sent them to the Congress of the USA to represent the people. Perhaps a dose of Lincoln's "honesty," is all that is needed to save the day. Wouldn't that be nice?

Our "honorables," do not even seem to care for our well-being. They care for their leadership positions, which make them big shots, and they care for themselves for sure. Unfortunately, they just can't get it into their heads that we the people are the reason they are in their positions of high stature in the first place.

We the people are the employers of all members of Congress, and they serve at our pleasure. The Constitution says so and the Bill of rights specifically enforces the people's power. The more we all understand that the tighter the reins we can place on errant politicians, the more the people are in charge. It is not too late. The Constitution and the Bill of Rights serve as our guide and they are our license to rid ourselves of a poor government, including the honorable so and so from such and such.

We must understand the Constitution and the Bill of Rights in order for them to work again for US and for America. The last thing we should consider doing is to permit the dirty politicians that we unfortunately have already elected to serve the people indefinitely. They are on track to disembody our Constitution through legislation and through executive actions aimed right at the heart of America.

Of course, a lot of the problem is our fault since we are too good--too trusting. We do not check them out well enough before we slam them into office for poor reasons such as their ads are good or because Blankety-Blank endorses them. Or worse than anything, we elect them because they promised us something for ourselves or for our families.

To make it simple to understand this notion—if there is a rotten piece of fish in the market and we select it for dinner, whose fault is it when it doesn't taste so good and our guests get sick? So, when we pick a rotten person to represent US—whose fault is that? You see, we do not have to be dummies. We simply choose to be.

Some politicians actually admit they operate for the money. Though they are few and far between. Some deny it even when it is obvious. For instance, Tom Corbett, Pennsylvania's friendly former governor, mysteriously collected $1.7 million from oil and gas companies but assured voters that "The contributions don't affect my decisions." Who was he kidding?

Here are some great facts from "Yes, We're Corrupt" by John Schwartz from theintercept.com on July 30, 2015. Politicians and donors vehemently deny being cooked and while they are lying their friends are out extolling their virtues.

For example, New York Times columnist David Brooks is quoted as follows: "Don't Follow the Money." Humph! Freakonomics co-author Stephen Dubner on public radio's Marketplace shouts out "Money does not buy elections." Humph again! Yale Law School professor Peter H. Schuck in the Los Angeles Times proudly cautions: "Money won't buy you votes" Hah! Right!

Despite these big-time liars preaching that the system is clean, regular Americans do not agree. In fact, 85 percent of Americans say we need to either "completely rebuild" or make "fundamental changes" to the campaign finance system. A mere 13 percent think "only minor changes are necessary." Hard as it is to believe this 13 percent is even less than the 18 percent of Americans who believe they have been in the presence of a ghost.

Harder for any of us to believe, there are actual politicians out there who acknowledge the glaringly obvious reality of such political corruption. We highlight a few below. On everybody's list of honest confessions is the short tale told by Donald Trump in the GOP debates of how easy he has been with his cash. We covered this before as it is classic but we must remember that when he was the perpetrator here, he had never been a politician so we forgive him this one time. In the same breath as his confession, then candidate Trump nailed all seventeen Republican candidates for president on the stage with him as "political takers," with this one statement:

"I gave to many people, before this, before two months ago, I was a businessman. I give to everybody. When they call, I give. And do you know what? When I need something from them two years later, three years later, I call them, they are there for me. And that's a broken system." — Donald Trump in 2015.

"This is what's wrong. [Donald Trump] buys and sells politicians of all stripes … he's used to buying politicians." — Sen. Rand Paul, R-Ky., in 2015.

"Now [the United States is] just an oligarchy, with unlimited political bribery being the essence of getting the nominations for president or to elect the president. And the same thing applies to governors and U.S. senators and congress members. ... So now we've just seen a complete subversion of our political system as a payoff to major contributors ..." — Jimmy Carter, former president, in 2015.

"The millionaire class and the billionaire class increasingly own the political process, and they own the politicians that go to them for money. ... we are moving very, very quickly from a democratic society, one person, one vote, to an oligarchic form of society, where billionaires would be determining who the elected officials of this country are." — Sen. Bernie Sanders, I-Vt., in 2015.

Another Sanders quote: "I think many people have the mistaken impression that Congress regulates Wall Street. ... The real truth is that Wall Street regulates the Congress."

"You have to go where the money is. Now where the money is, there's almost always implicitly some string attached. ... It's awful hard to take a whole lot of money from a group you know has a particular position then you conclude they're wrong and you vote no." — Vice President Joe Biden in 2015.

Today's whole political game, run by an absurdist's nightmare of moneyed elites, is ridiculous – a game in which corporations are people and money is magically empowered to speak; candidates trek to the corporate suites and secret retreats of the rich, shamelessly selling their political souls." – Jim Hightower, former Democratic agricultural commissioner of Texas, 2015.

This is just a sampling of those people who are brave or stupid enough to acknowledge that politicians sell their immortal souls for political gain which includes campaign cash. It sure does make them dirty and corrupt and the sooner we get them all out of office after electing them, the better.

Does it really matter whether the government is controlled by Democrats or Republicans? Democratic leaders have become socialist progressives, just this side of communists over the past several years. The regular Democrats at home are not far leftists but their leaders do not look at anything ideologically the way the people do.

Republicans still seem to love the American way publicly and are not overtly moving the country towards communism. But, wimpy Republicans are not as active enough in their opposition to the Democrats as they should be. Our country's rate of demise grows at a faster clip when leftist progressive communists are in office. When Republicans take over, though it lessens, it does go to zero as it should because a number of Republicans have become progressive also. That is not good!

So, right now at least, Republicans, especially conservative Republicans are a better choice for America than Democrats. As a conservative Democrat myself, that is very tough for me to say. I wish it were not so. The best thing for America is for citizens to vote for conservatives, nationalists, and populists as loving America is a good thing. With conservatives lying to their base all the time recently, I would say vote for a good person even if they are Democrat. The facts show most conservatives are either Republican or Libertarian but more and more are nationalists and or populists who simply love America.

The people somehow are always short changed on the notion of representation and honesty. Honesty is the first thing to go when a representative must lie in order to get the extra benefits their positions can deliver.

When has any incumbent representative run effectively on honesty? Is that because we the people do not care about honesty or are we all smart enough to know that they are kidding. We do not need the Constitution to know that but it might help us all to be more honest if we knew and loved the Constitution and its Bill of Rights just a little bit more.

Can we blame politicians if we elect them simply because our nephews will do well with them do well? In these cases, we must blame ourselves. Either way it is our fault. We voted most of these 545 miscreants into office to run our government. We get the government we deserve.

Somebody once said that if you like your honesty, you will be able to keep it and it should save you about $2500.00 per year. But I jest, yet my jest is serious. Do you know who that guy was? Now, helping fight a guy like that is a great place in which we can use our knowledge of the Bill of Rights and the even greater rights provided by the US Constitution.

OK, nobody said that exactly but some president at some time in his last eight-year term lied through his teeth and told Americans that they could keep their doctors, their health policies, and they could pocket $2500.00. I am not kidding. He is still telling lies in the deep state almost a year after he was voted out simply because no person in Congress felt strong enough to buck the low information gullible American people and take him on.

Now with President Trump on their side, they still won't take on Obama notions that the people have detested for eight years. These wimps must be defeated by those of us who want a strong America.

There is a chasm. We the people can fix the chasm. Learning the precepts of the Bill of Rights, expanded further by the inherent rights in the Constitution and the Declaration of Independence, can inspire US to get that task done.

My objective with this book is to help smarten up all Americans so that guys like that, whether they are the past president or not, do not get to treat any of us like chumps. Each time I write about this topic, I get smarter also as we all must keep learning and we must be watchful of tyranny so that we can keep our freedoms and our liberties. If you had a choice, to which of your favorite politicians would you give your freedom and liberty so they could continually get reelected?

America is built on fairness, goodness, and individual strength. We (the people) are not supposed to give politicians an even break. The Constitution is our law and it is our obligation to pay attention so our rights are not violated by grabby self-centered dirty politicians. If you happen to be in this low information / overly nice category, thank you for visiting this book. I hope that through these writings, you will become a better American.

The low information gullible people in America must smarten up or we are lost. Everybody's vote counts the same. When those, who choose to not pay attention vote, it is a big plus for dirty politicians and a big loss for real Americans.

When you have the time, please finish reading this book, and you will understand how smart you can be and how much power you can wield against those who care nothing about you or me, or America. Always keep your eye on the ball and do not give the ball up to an opponent just because they lie and they schmooze you.

This classic book is written so that we can all know the truth even when the corrupt national media lies to our faces as they do every day. The not-so-free, very dishonest and corrupt statist press provides propaganda for the government and too many gullible Americans sop it up as if it is the truth.

The media would have us all believe in the "*Tooth Fairy.*" Any of US that live by believing their lies, are simply un-smartened chumps. A 50-cent piece of chocolate replacing a missing tooth makes this travesty no better.

Unfortunately, too many look to government, the creators of all American problems, as the only place where a problem can be solved. Not true! Never go to a problem creator for a solution!

When I was growing up, it was not this way. It is time that we went back to the better days when there was a real American Dream for everybody, not just children from Mexico.

What happened to America and Americans first? I hope this book as all others that I have written in my undocumented patriotic series helps to wake up Americans of all ages from the fog that has affected the brains of many who would be otherwise would be declared smart.

We have not changed but we have permitted our government to change. Our representatives and our government have changed so much that they have forgotten who we are and who we the people are supposed to be.

Nobody really expected a positive fundamental change in America from the past president who promised a fundamental change. Most of us thought he was talking about patching a pretty good system. Not so!

This past president never seemed very overjoyed about being an American. He spent eight years trying to eliminate America and to create a communist socialist state in its stead. More and more Americans, now that we have a president in whom we can believe, think this fundamental change had nothing to do with making America better, and it was not the change for which they voted.

Without using those exact words, our Constitution gives US a government *of the people, by the people, and for the people*. These exact words are used in the Declaration of Independence which was an operating precept when the Constitution was written.

The Bill of Rights specifically grants powers to the people which the government of the prior president, BHO, played like he wanted to take away. The Constitution, of which the Bill of Rights is an add-on part—but integral to the purpose for sure, gives government only the powers that are specifically enumerated by the people and no more. Leftists purposely misinterpret this thinking it gives government additional powers but it gives government, especially, the federal government nothing. Well, it does give a big message to get lost in the affairs of the people.

It is a shame that too many Americans have become indifferent and perhaps even lazy and we have permitted corrupt politicians to be reelected regardless of whether they represent US well or not. Shame on US!

Abraham Lincoln is the most famous historical figure to use this patriotic phrase. It was in his Gettysburg Address from November 19, 1863. For posterity, here is Lincoln's last paragraph. It is chilling:

"It is rather for us to be here dedicated to the great task remaining before us -- that from these honored dead we take increased devotion to that cause for which they gave the last full measure of devotion -- that we here highly resolve that these dead shall not have died in vain -- that this nation, under God, shall

have a new birth of freedom -- and that government of the people, by the people, for the people, shall not perish from the earth."

If I ask you to do anything besides pay attention in this book, it is to reject the fundamental changes that are destined to bring in a much bigger government—bigger than the population at large. Big government doesn't work.

Big agencies don't work. Big corporations don't work. Big doesn't work well at all, especially if you are one individual person looking for freedom and liberty. Your personal Bill of Rights does not require you to ever accept big over the will of the people.

Government has grown so big that we the people, who own the government according to a deed known as the Constitution, and some explicit notions such as The Bill of Rights can no longer sort through all the lies and the empty promises of government as put forth by the corrupt media. Government has simply gotten too big and too powerful for regular citizens. Government has already become the biggest bully in America. Why should we let it grow even bigger?

So, we must all help reduce the size of government for the people to ever matter again. We get our chances each election cycle. When we vote to favor corruption and the advocates of government growth, we get the government we deserve. They will be coming for us all!

If all Americans understood America, instead of blaming America first for everything—we would not have to worry about being defeated from within.

In this way, if any American political party led by Democrats or Republicans, wanted to change America into a Communist-Russian-like, or Communist-Chinese-like, or Nazi-German-like country, we would be better equipped to fire off a quick yet, or a mhai, or simply, a hearty and guttural nein! Some of us might simply say, "Buzz Off!"

If you believe in any of the leftist progressive socialist philosophies and you also like your freedom, it might be a good time to visit the tombstone makers in your area and pick out a good one. In memoriam! You are gone! Know your rights! Know the Bill of Rights!

Chapter 9 Bill of Rights Says: Throws the Bums Out!

Write opinion letters and call your representatives

The purpose of this book as noted from the beginning is to keep America as founded and to help US all be better Americans by understanding the Bill of Rights, an essential ingredient of the US Constitution. At the same time, as an adjunct to a greater understanding of our rights, we all need to learn a lot about America's founding. Most of us have heard of the Bill of Rights as an integral part of the US Constitution and when our rights are presented properly, we really like them. Who could say no to prosperity through liberty and freedom?

Many know the story of the Bill of Rights as it was actually an after-thought to the US Constitution—the defining document of our country. Doubtful patriots, who examined the Constitution for approval, wrote that all powers and rights not explicitly given to the government were held by the people. That means that the people own the government and not vice versa. So, let's say among other specific powers, the Constitution grants to the President, the Congress, and the Courts operating as the government the following powers / rights:

- ✓ To lay and collect import duties
- ✓ To pay the debts of the U.S. Government.
- ✓ To regulate commerce with foreign nations and Indian Tribes.
- ✓ To regulate commerce among the States.
- ✓ To regulate immigration
- ✓ To build roads and bridges
- ✓ To provide for the common defense (Army, Navy…), E
- ✓ Etc.

As you can see, these are things that we all would expect government to do as well as a number of other specific tasks all laid out in the Constitution. As you read the Constitution for free on the Internet or by a book by this author, you will notice that certain rights for government are not included; such as:

- ✓ Killing Citizens.
- ✓ Preventing the people from assembling in groups of more than two.
- ✓ Demanding that the people shop only at government stores.
- ✓ Requiring men to shave
- ✓ Preventing the people from eating on Tuesday.
- ✓ Etc.

This quote from the Tenth Amendment of the Bill of Rights applies regarding government powers as follows:

The powers not delegated to the United States by the Constitution, nor prohibited by it to the States, are reserved to the States respectively, or to the people.

Only the rights specifically given to government in the Constitution are in government's purview. All other rights are reserved for the people. In other words, the people have all other powers and rights than those specifically given to government. Don't be fooled otherwise.

Any power not listed in the Constitution specifically, says the Tenth Amendment, is left to the states or the people. Although the Tenth Amendment does not specify what these "powers" may be, the U.S. Supreme Court has ruled that laws affecting family relations (such as marriage, divorce, and adoption), commerce that occurs within a state's own borders, and local law enforcement activities, are among those specifically reserved to the states or the people.

Since the Constitution gives almost all rights and powers to the people, there was disagreement among many of the founders and the citizens of the 1780's about the Constitution outlining specifically all the rights of the people. There was a difference of opinion and the Bill of Rights ultimately arrived after the Constitution was ratified to clarify the intent of the founders on the matter of government powers and state's rights.

The majority of the founders believed that by saying the people have all rights other than those reserved for government, as they wrote in The Constitution, and the government had only those rights specifically mentioned, that should have been enough. What more should we have needed?

To repeat, the Constitution as written from the beginning already provided all rights the people would ever put in a Bill of Rights, and the government was given its specific powers so it could function as a government.

Though this is not how it actually works, let's try this exercise to get a better understanding of our rights v. government rights.

Rather than saying the people have all rights not explicitly granted by the people to the government, let's suppose that the founders tried to define every single right / power for all Americans. In this process, let's say they numbered the rights beginning with number 1.

Suppose when all the rights were listed and added to the Constitution, the number of rights was calculated to be, say, 437. What would happen if in trying to define the 437 rights, which in this scenario the founders believed all Americans should possess, they forgot a right or just a part of right? Then what? What if this particular right's number just happened to be 93? Then what?

In this fictitious scenario of 437 rights and no more, to make our point, as noted, the Constitution as written provides not just for right number 93, but all rights from zero to 437 but no additional rights. Anything beyond 437 if listed would be a power of the government by default. Again, this is a fictitious example but the point is that this could have been an alternative way of granting rights that would be very specific with numbered rights and no global rights permitted.

To clarify further, the people in this fictitious scenario did not have global rights. They had all rights defined from zero to 437 but none others and no parts that were forgotten and not specified. Anything that was forgotten in a specific right was not a right.

To say again, anything that would be a right of the people would have to be specified within the 437 defined rights or it would not be a right / power of the people. Government would have its listed powers and rights as well as discussed above but rights not listed for the people would be in the government column. Does that sound better than the people having all the rights except those they place in the government's column?

As you might suspect, there would be a problem when a missing right were needed, once the Constitution was finalized. The problem would occur when the people sought to have a right number 438, about which nobody ever would have conceived when the rights were originally numbered to 437?

What if enough people were pro-government that they would not vote the people to have the additional rights or to have right # 93 amended to add the forgotten clause? It could create a big problem for the people. It would give the government the greater hand over the people's hand.

It helps to remember that the founders in forming the US government are the same group that seceded from England because England had all the rights. They fought a revolution to gain all the rights that were natural for the people to possess. They were not about to give government any loopholes in which government could claim power over the people that were not fully intended by the founders.

And, so the default is that the states, aka the people, got the rights and the federal government got the enumerated powers—only those powers specifically listed in the Constitution.

So, what did the founders do so there would not be conflicts of new rights or parts of rights that were not specifically noted? at this would never happen?

1. The constitution specifically lists all of government's rights / powers.
2. All other rights are granted to the people.

3. A Bill of Rights was added to the Constitution for the people—though the Bill of rights is redundant since the Constitution already grants all rights not reserved for government to the people.
4. Since a new right is already granted by the Constitution, rights do not have to be granted specifically and were not often granted after the Bill of Rights was devised and ratified.
5. Despite this great compromise, only ten of the twelve rights proposed were ratified; and since that time, just seventeen changes were made to the constitution in the form of amendments—the same form in which the Bill of Rights were presented.

The Constitution and its 27 amendments including the Bill of Rights is the place to go to find out what America is all about! It is about the U.S. of A.—our nation. Our Country is what it is because its definition is embodied in its Constitution, which is America's most fundamental prized set of laws. The Bill of Rights and all other Constitutional changes (amendments) together with the base Constitution represent the total body of the Constitution.

To say it again for clarity, all amendments to the Constitution, especially the first ten known as the Bill of Rights, are in fact part of the Constitution. They are not adjuncts to it in function; though they are in form. And thus, the Bill of Rights, the topic of this book is a major part of the Constitution. It is not a bunch of independent precepts brought forth to make us all feel better about life.

Our job, as Americans moving through life of course, is to learn what we can about our government (as defined by the Constitution—including the Bill of Rights et al.). In this endeavor, we should all pay attention that our Congressional representatives actually spend their time representing US according to the laws of the founders, who, if they had their way, would never let US down.

When our representatives do not do the will of the people in-between elections we must remember that they represent US, not the government. We need to write letters to the editors of newspapers and other media, and write our Congressmen and Senators so they know they cannot snooker us, and so they know who is the boss—we the people.

If they don't listen, then we must do the honorable thing and write them even more letters, and letters to the editors of popular newspapers, and if and when they choose not to respond in our favor, or worse than that, they do not respond at all, we then must un-elect these leaders their next time out on the ballot.

Un-elect them! They would hate it!

Unfortunately for Americans, our representative in the Congress, the Supreme Court, and the Presidency is not Jefferson Smith from the movie *Mr. Smith Goes to Washington*. His honor is impeccable. But, the honor of our representatives in the twenty-first century has become very tarnished and quite questionable.

Do they represent US or do they represent themselves? Do they represent corporations or special interests? If our representatives are doing their jobs, why is our country messed up so badly that it may be irreparable as Congress cannot or will not work together for the good of the people.

When our country is handed over to non-citizens by our representatives, have they represented the citizens of the USA? When a president addresses unescorted children from Central America and he tells them they are the future of America, what is he really telling the children of American citizens?

Our representation has been getting progressively worse each year—not better. Over the past few years, especially from 2009 through 2016, with the healthcare debacle and open borders topping the list of domestic travails, it is clear that the voices of the people were not being heard in Washington, DC.

The government of the past administration seemingly every day weakened our opportunity to survive as it cut and health services that we need and then it cut again. None of us want a corrupt government deciding if we live or die or what health services we can get or not get. Government should make no decisions regarding the healthcare of an individual person.

Just as Jefferson Smith in the Frank Capra classic movie, *Mr. Smith Goes to Washington*, found out, the corrupt purposes of elected officials are now in the open. It is to serve themselves by serving special interests. During the past administration, government officials have been emboldened to steal away rights from the people to better suit the government.

Because government does not have the right or the power to do this, these recent actions have been unconstitutional. Simply by being unconstitutional does not fix the usurpation of power. Instead, the government making such bad choices must be replaced by a government that will reinstate the power of the people. And. The people's ultimate power is to replace representation that has gone bad.

In the sunlight of the day, therefore, the existing Congress—yes, both houses, must go. Not the institution of Congress, just the corrupt members who choose not to serve the people.

We must bid them sayonara. We must say adieu. We must sign off with a big adios. Our right to do this comes directly from the Constitution, not from the Bill of Rights—but the Tenth Amendment emphasizes the rights of all Americans to run America. It is a right of all Americans to un-elect the scoundrels that rip our country apart.

And when it comes time to elect our next President, and our next Congress; let's not forget to bring in an honest person who loves America as much as we do. Many feels that President Donald Trump fits that description but Congress still has not gotten the people's message. If the mess we had during the past president's tenure, if it were not the president's intentions, and the president's direct fault, then whose fault, I might ask, was it?

Might it have been Stanley Laurel's or Oliver Hardy's—for it surely is a comedy!! It was President Barack H. Obama and he is gone, and many of us say, Thank God! Others of course miss his unconstitutional executive orders. But, they are not friends of an America created by our founders.

Today's surprise

When I wrote this paragraph originally before the last presidential election, I got a surprise. I was shopping at Malacari's, a great produce market in Wilkes-Barre PA, frequented by poorer people and smart shoppers. I am so glad Malacari's is in Wilkes-Barre.

When I was joking around with the checkout person and the person behind me; I admitted that I was unemployed (Most writers are unemployed until their works are sold.), but I did not say I was writing books hoping the big one would come in. Hah!

I said lightly that I was thinking about running for President but that it seemed that everybody was so happy with the current President that I figured I should look someplace else for a new ob. I then said that everybody loves him so much, I would not have a chance anyway.

The Cashier stopped in her tracks and said: "that may have been a while ago but you should check again as it is not that way now." The lady behind her said that she "did not think anybody liked him anymore." I admit, I was surprised. After getting news from the media for eight years and not changing my circle of friends, I was clearly out of touch.

I have Democrat-loving can't do any wrong relatives in my family who are still doing well and they still were deeply in love with the past president. So, I figured the past president was still doing OK. But, when these Jane Q Publics at the store check-out line told me they were retired and collecting and still felt they had to work until they died, I started to think maybe you can't fool all of the people all of the time.

I was very surprised. As we examine the notions that come our way, isn't that why you are reading this book? Thank you to all the Americans ready to fight for American values. We need more of you today in our America! "Don't give up the ship." Keep firing until America wins.

You may know that about a year into the War of 1812, the first full scale war for the new America after the Revolution, Captain James Lawrence said these heroic words after being mortally wounded. It was in the engagement between his ship, the U.S. frigate Chesapeake, and the HMS Shannon on June 1, 1813. While the wounded Lawrence was being carried below, his duty for his ship and his love for America motivated him to order his officers: "Tell the men to fire faster! Don't give up the ship!"

Keep firing until America wins. Use the Bill of Rights, the Constitution, and all great American principles as your ammunition.

Chapter 10 The Declaration of Rights and Grievances

The First Document on the way to the American Revolution

Let's go back in time to right before the American Revolution. Before we wholesale study the Bill of Rights and the good it has done for America, let's take a trip back so that we all understand the many documents that came before this famous declaration of rights.

Ironically, long before the Bill of Rights, in fact, even before the outset of the Revolutionary War, one of the first documents on the way to the Declaration of Independence and The Constitution was the Declaration of Rights and Grievances. This is not the Bill of Rights, but it surely set the stage for American independence.

This declaration was a product of the First Continental Congress. The colonists were upset with foreign rule from England because they were not given a real voice in the government. As an aside, unfortunately not much has changed for regular American citizens since that time, as the set of officials in Washington through the last administration and even our current Congress have no problem stealing rights from the people.

As a point of note, all of the founding documents that we discuss are available for free on the Internet. They are also available in hard copy in many books including your author's popular book titled, *Taxation Without Representation.*

The Declaration of Rights and Grievances was the first formal request of the "United States" to England for a return to representative government. The colonists were seeking a return to a form of government as had originally been established by the Crown. The demands of the colonists were not outlandish.

Though nothing close to a constitutional democracy, the colonists under English rule enjoyed representation in the lower house of all of the colonial "state" governments.

There was no union of colonies or states at the time and had the English kept to themselves and not levied taxes directly on the colonists, Americans today would be much more interested if Camilla is really ever going to be the Queen.

With a careful reading of the Declaration of Rights and Grievances, one can get a quick sense of what the colonists wanted from the Crown. It was simply, "no taxation without representation," and all of the many positions this plea represented. As the thought of a revolution became more of a reality for the patriots, independence and freedom and liberty became even more important than the tax burden.

This early declaration was the first major document of the new government of the United States, though it occurred at a time when the states were not actively seeking independence from the Crown.

The expressed purpose of the First Continental Congress held in 1774 was:

"That a Committee be appointed to state the rights of the Colonies in general, the several instances in which these rights are violated or infringed, and the means most proper to be pursued for obtaining a restoration of them."

The committee was constructed and the declaration was drafted and it was read on September 22nd and the draft of the grievances was read on the 24th. The members of the First Congress debated the drafts on October 12 and 13, and after a final draft was produced, it was agreed on Friday, October 14, 1774.

At this First Continental Congress, the delegates drafted several documents, and several drafts of documents, one of which was the document known as The Declaration of Rights and Grievances. This was the statement of American complaints agreed to on October 14, 1774.

The document was sent to King George III, to whom, at the time, many of the delegates remained loyal. It was not sent to Parliament since the delegates did not have the same level of loyalty to this body. Quite frankly, the document implored King George III to step in and rescue the colonies from the English Parliament.

The radical colonial delegates (aka patriots) were critical of this particular declaration because it continued to concede the right of Parliament to regulate colonial trade, a view that was losing favor in the mid-1770s. Many suggest that the actual cause of the American Revolution is found in this major historical document.

Chapter 11 The Articles of Association

Dear King George III

Several days after the signing and sending of the Declaration of Rights and Grievances to England, on October 20, 1774, the First Continental Congress passed the Articles of Association. They had been written during the same Congress. The Congress, by the way was the colonial Congress (First Continental Congress) and not the Congress of today. There was no House and no Senate for these institutions of representation today were created by The US Constitution. The Constitution was about thirteen years away at this time in history.

Ironically in the modern era, progressive communists operate freely in the press and the Democratic Party. Their objective is to do away with the entire Constitution. For years, they had a majority in the Senate and a President to help them in this traitorous cause, but they failed. Nonetheless they will try again and even today, they try to unseat our duly elected president for no cause but their own desire to undue the laws of the founders.

Ironically, they have all received their power to exist—raison d 'etre—from the same Constitution that these dirty politicians in the Executive and Legislative branches hold in such disdain.

As with the Declaration of Rights and Grievances, the Articles of Association were also addressed to King George III. In essence, it was a formal agreement of the colonies themselves to work together as an association of states with common purpose. How King George would react to such demands was an interesting consideration. The colonist patriots were extremely brave men.

It was basically a union of protest and boycott as many of the articles in the document which outlined the specifications that the colonists were to take regarding the export and import of goods.

When you read these articles, you can't help but notice the elegance and forethought in the draft. We are a fortunate lot indeed to have had such fine and capable, and yes, honorable men, representing America in our founding days.

Both the Declaration of Rights and Grievances as discussed in the prior chapter as well as the Articles of Association, were prompted substantially by the Coercive Acts of Parliament enacted in the 1774-time frame.

The Coercive Acts by Parliament included the following:

1. The Boston Port Act closed the port of Boston until damages from the Boston Tea Party were paid.

2. The Massachusetts Government Act restricted Massachusetts; democratic town meetings and turned the governor's council into an appointed body.

3. The Administration of Justice Act made British officials immune to criminal prosecution in Massachusetts.

4. The Quartering Act revisited from 1765, required colonists to house and quarter British troops on demand, including in their private homes as a last resort.

5. The Quebec Act. Though not technically part of the Coercive Acts, the colonists lumped a fifth act, known as the Quebec Act along with the four Coercive acts into a set of five that they referred to as "The Intolerable Acts." The Quebec Act extended freedom of worship to Catholics in Canada, as well as granting Canadians the continuation of their judicial system. Religious tolerance at the time was not at its best. The mainly Protestant colonists did not look kindly on the ability of Catholics to worship freely on their borders.

When you have a chance, you should consider taking a look at the Articles of Association in Appendix B as another major document that helps define the American thought process before America was ready to take up arms against England.

Because sometimes the long paragraphs of the founders, though quite eloquent, put regular Americans to sleep. You might consider checking out The Constitution by Hamilton, Jefferson, and Madison, edited by your author for a more cohesive treatment. Just as in this book I have parsed some material to be more readable without removing any words or meaning.

Another great source of information and also easy to read is Sol Bloom's Epoch … Story of the Constitution, which has recently been re-mastered and refined and re-published by Lets Go Publish! (LGP). It too is available on amazon.com/author/brianwkelly.

The Articles of Association are worth reading for sure.

History of the Articles of Association

God bless all the signers of the Articles of Association from all the thirteen states of the first union. A brave lot they were for sure. Where were brave Americans in the past administration? Even the Republicans in Congress wimped out. It seems many today are sleeping as our country is in deep peril once again. The opposition is trying again to beat us by disarming us. Keep your guns, please! And do not let them disparage President Trump in your presence.

The Articles of Association were written while the colonies hoped they could work out a deal with Britain so that freedom did not have to come from war. As a side note, the Brits knew the brave colonists were armed, and so even the mighty English walked gingerly in the colonies.

As you can see by reading the Articles of Association, this document calls on the colonies to stop importing goods from the British Isles beginning on December 1, 1774, if the Coercive Acts were not repealed.

You may enjoy checking out the coercive acts (aka to some as the Intolerable Acts). Though it is not the thrust of this book, by reading the very short historical synopsis in this chapter, presented above, you can get a sense of the items that were most upsetting to the colonists.

Should Britain fail to redress the colonists' grievances in a timely manner, this First Congress declared, then it would reconvene on May 10, 1775, and the colonies would cease to export goods to Britain on September 10, 1775. After proclaiming these measures, the First Continental Congress disbanded on October 26, 1774.

Have you ever seen America so decisive? For me, the closest time other than this was the Cuban Missile Crisis! Bravo JFK!

Colonial Americans loved America and could not believe the British were going to hurt any American who wanted real freedom. They understood why the British were upset by the Boston Tea Party and other blatant acts of destruction of supposedly British property by American colonists. Yet, the colonists did not condone the British Acts, which eventually forced America's hand.

Still thinking that the Americans would do whatever was demanded, the British Parliament enacted the very nasty Coercive Acts, as previously discussed, much to the outrage of American patriots, on March 28, 1774.

Historians know that the Coercive Acts were a series of four acts established by the British government. The aim of the legislation was to restore order from the Crown's perspective in Massachusetts and to punish Bostonians big-time for their "Tea Party."

The British saw this "Tea Party" as an emboldened act by the revolutionary-minded Sons of Liberty, who had boarded three British Tea Ships in Boston Harbor and dumped 342 crates of tea—nearly $1 million worth in today's money—into the water to protest the British Tea Act.

Since life had not improved for the British, who had become money-strapped, after initially backing off from its taxation impositions, they began to double down on the colonists. They continued to impose their will on the colonists.

Seeing it coming, Americans were ready for action. The Second Continental Congress began on May 10, 1775 and it went on until March 1, 1781. It was well in session during the Revolutionary War. Yes, the colonists, brave everyday folks as they were, took up arms against a super-power!

During the Revolutionary War, the Second Congress of the US continued, but its meeting location was moved from Philadelphia several times to other locations to protect the lives of the representatives.

Britain, as an adversary was not an easy foe with which to deal. The Americans needed to smarten up on the battlefield and so they looked for great generals. They found George Washington.

The English considered the American Revolution as tyranny, while the patriots in the colonies saw England's imposition of its strength upon the colonies as a tyrannical act that Americans could not tolerate.

The delegates from twelve of the thirteen original colonies gathered again in Philadelphia to discuss their next steps in dealing with England. This Second Congress met at the State House in Philadelphia (Now popularly known as Independence Hall) as the American Revolution had already begun in earnest with the shot heard round the world still ringing in their ears.

After major deliberations in Georgia, this last colony finally joined the Congress, dispatching delegates who arrived on July 20, 1775.

When the Second Continental Congress came together on May 10, 1775 it was, in effect, a reconvening of the First Continental Congress. The Colonies sent many of the same 56 delegates who attended the first meeting. They appointed the same president (Peyton Randolph) and secretary (Charles Thomson). Some now famous new arrivals to Congress included Benjamin Franklin of Pennsylvania and John Hancock of Massachusetts.

Peyton Randolph, the President of Congress, a very important person in Virginia Politics, was summoned back to Virginia unexpectedly to preside over the House of Burgesses within two weeks of the convening of the 2nd Congress. Virginia sent Thomas Jefferson, and another brave historical figure, to replace him. Jefferson arrived several weeks later.

Henry Middleton was elected as President of Congress to replace Randolph, but he declined. John Hancock was then elected President of the Congress on May 24, 1775. One might say that John Hancock was the 2nd President of the United States (Peyton Randolph was the first) at a time when the country operated without a Constitution. As you will see, the Constitution, which created a new government, created a new Congress and a lot more.

Massachusetts, which appears to have been the toughest state at the time, (turned wimpy over the years) much differently than the Massachusetts of today, had already organized the Minutemen. This was a special militia that could be ready on a minute's notice.

Minutemen skirmished with British troops at Lexington and Concord. Meanwhile, other farmer-soldiers joined them outside Boston to fight for America. The militia was still engaged in Boston while the Congress was using its powers to formally establish the Massachusetts militia as the Continental Army of the United States with George Washington of Virginia as the top general.

The head of this army was known at the time as the Commander in Chief. And this general with the power won America its rights before America needed a Bill of Rights.

This marked another stage in the formation of the government of the US. The government would continue to evolve and after independence was gained, George Washington would again become Commander in Chief when he was elected First President of the United States.

Sixty-five representatives originally appointed to the Second Continental Congress by the legislatures of thirteen British North American colonies accomplished a body of work that is historical in nature. At the time, it formed the basis for the new government, ready to take on and defeat England.

The Declaration of Independence, available with all of the founders' documents on the Internet for free, was the first well-known historical document produced by this Second Congress. The second was the Articles of Confederation.

All of this great documentation of the strife of the colonists in their relationship with Britain is put forth in all of these documents, the intent of which at the time was to make America free from England. The Articles of Confederation was the pre-cursor document to the United States Constitution. Both are freely available on the Internet.

As noted previously, the Second Continental Congress was convened during the American Revolutionary War but prior to July 4, 1776. It served as the de facto U.S. national government as there was nothing else on the colonist side, as powerful. This Continental Congress assumed power and raised armies, directed strategy, appointed diplomats, and it made the US government a formal entity. Was it not amazing? Think about all that could have gone wrong. But, because of bravery and determination for freedom and liberty, it did not go wrong.

At the same time, this Congress of America's finest founders, produced numerous important documents, including two of the most fundamental and historical documents to American freedom—*The Declaration of Independence and The Articles of Confederation.* Both of these documents led to the creation of the US Constitution in 1787.

Chapter 12 The US Declaration of Independence

By the Second Congress, July 4, 1776

You can see the agita rising as one document after another, showed the colonists placing simple requests from England for rights the colonists for years believed they already had.

Some dates, one can never forget. The Declaration of Independence was written by Thomas Jefferson, a relative newcomer to the list of patriots and a real youngster, and it was put forth and approved for printing on July 4, 1776. It was a product of the Second Continental Congress. It did exactly what it purported to do in its title. It declared independence from Great Britain.

It was not Pennsylvania, or Massachusetts or Virginia that declared this independence and this is a key point. Instead, it was all of the thirteen colonies in unison, known to themselves as states at the time. They had chosen to assemble and join in a union to create a new federal government that would soon become known as the United States of America.

Once independence was declared, even though the fighting was underway, America began to legally operate fully independent of the Crown with its own government. Considering that the colonists were in revolt and war had commenced, it is an understatement to suggest that the colonists were not operating independently prior to the Declaration. The Declaration formalized their union of independence, and for those thinking that England still ruled the day, it solidified America as the major power.

If you are willing to fight for your statements, you can state anything. The colonists were ready to fight, and had in fact begun the fight!

The states were declared to be free and independent and "all political connection between them and the State of Great Britain, is and ought to be totally dissolved."

The formal title of the document ratified on July 4, 1776 is the "**Unanimous Declaration of the thirteen United States of America**," but to Americans it is known simply as the Declaration of Independence. This was the formal end of the thirteen colonies and the beginning of the United States of America!

Declaration of Independence – Explanation and Additional Thoughts

In addition to declaring independence, this document gave justification for the separation from the Crown in sufficient detail that the King and Parliament could not misunderstand its purpose and from whence it came. Since the colonies were no more, historians consider this Declaration as the founding document of the United States of America. In his Gettysburg Address of 1863, at the beginning of his address, President Lincoln memorialized the founding of the United States in these words:

Four score and seven years ago our fathers brought forth on this continent, a new nation, conceived in liberty, and dedicated to the proposition that all men are created equal.

And so, though some contest it, as the founding document; the Declaration of Independence still is in effect. Along with the essence of the Constitution and the ninth amendment (in the Bill of Rights) it gives the rights to the people, including rights not discovered at the time of the writing of the amendments.

As we know from our knowledge of American History and its recount of the Revolutionary War, there were a number of battles until the Americans prevailed in the war with England. After the Declaration of Independence, the Second Continental Congress stayed in session, meeting periodically, passing laws and drafting other documents that ultimately would define the new nation as the United States of America.

The next major document in the formation of the government of the United States is known as The Articles of Confederation. These Articles served as the defining document of rules until a "more perfect union" was formed with the writing and the adoption of the US Constitution. Until the Constitution, the Articles of Confederation were the Law of the Land.

Chapter 13 The Articles of Confederation

Written and adopted by the Second Congress, November 15, 1777

While the Revolutionary War was still in progress, the Second Continental Congress adopted the Articles of Confederation, the first "constitution" of the United States, on November 15, 1777. However, ratification of the Articles of Confederation by all thirteen states did not occur until March 1, 1781.

Thus, it can be concluded that the whole revolution was prosecuted without benefit of a "perfect" national set of laws. Having a Congress of the states in session filled in for the lack of a formal national body of law during this time. The Articles of Confederation, "approval in process" served as the model, which Congress used to govern the new United States. There were about two years left in the wary of independence when the articles of confederation became the law of the land.

Just as the Declaration of Independence is short for a longer title, the "Articles of Confederation and Perpetual Union" has been shortened over time to be simply The Articles of Confederation. Some say that the Articles of Confederation represent the United States of America's first constitution. After the Second Continental Congress, the Articles established a "firm league of friendship," which is affirmed as a not too trivial perpetual union between and among the 13 about-to-be-united states.

After having been subjected to the wiles of the strong central government of the British prior to the War of Independence, these Articles reflect a sense of the wariness by the states of a government that would not provide them with their God-given rights.

The Articles are the agreed-upon remedy for the concerns of states' rights and for individual rights. Ever fearful that a government of the future (such as the prior regime in the US or one hence) might not have the right measure of concern for our individual needs and rights if it were given too much power, and that abuses such as the Intolerable Acts, might again be the result, the Articles purposely established a guiding set of rules / laws, which in essence was a "constitution." It surely served the purposes of this fledgling government.

The full contents of the Articles of Confederation and all the founding documents are available on the Internet or in many hard cover books such as those by your author at www.amazon.com/author/brianwkelly.

They looked like this inside:

ARTICLES
OF
CONFEDERATION
AND
PERPETUAL UNION
BETWEEN
THE
STATES
OF
NEW HAMPSHIRE, MASSACHUSETTS-BAY RHODE ISLAND AND PROVIDENCE PLANTATIONS, CONNECTICUT, NEW YORK, NEW JERSEY, PENNSYLVANIA, DELAWARE, MARYLAND, VIRGINIA, NORTH CAROLINA, SOUTH CAROLINA AND GEORGIA

WILLIAMSBURG:
Printed by Alexander Purdie

Now, here is how a copy of how the cover looked many years after it was printed:

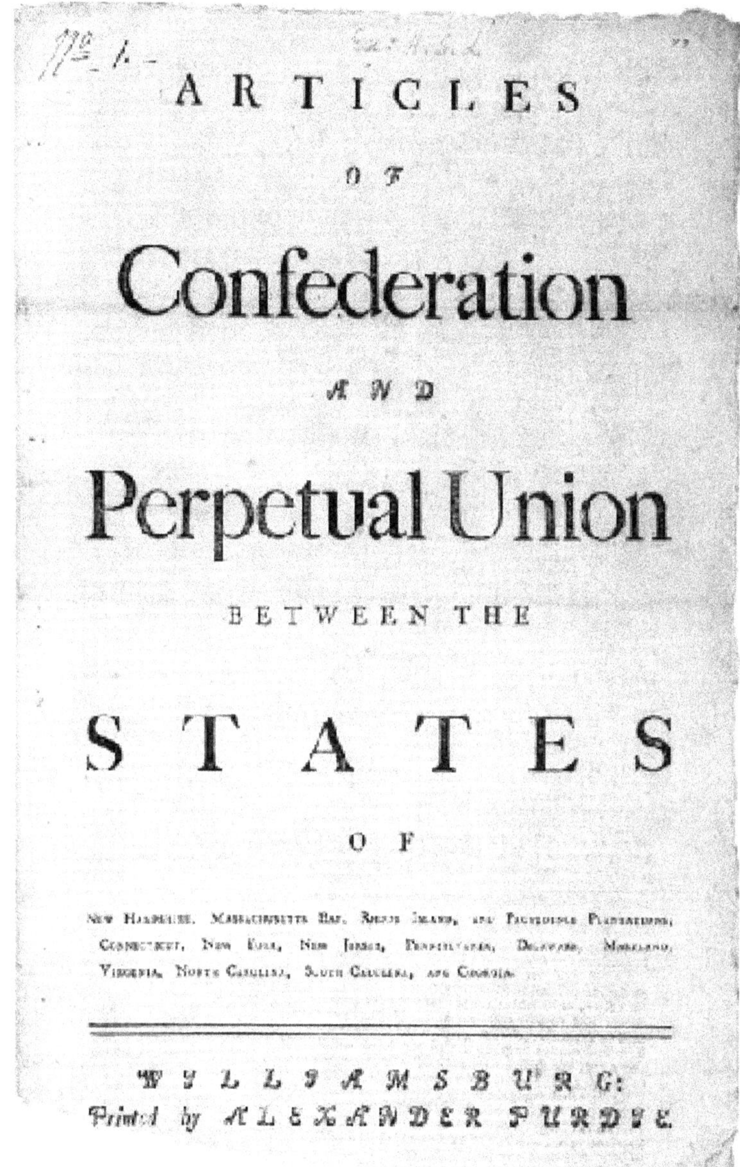

ARTICLES

OF

Confederation

AND

Perpetual Union

BETWEEN THE

STATES

OF

New Hampshire, Massachusetts Bay, Rhode Island, and Providence Plantations, Connecticut, New York, New Jersey, Pennsylvania, Delaware, Maryland, Virginia, North Carolina, South Carolina, and Georgia.

WILLIAMSBURG:
Printed by ALEXANDER PURDIE.

Take a Look!

When analyzed correctly, the Articles of Confederation vested the largest share of US power to the individual states. When the Constitution was built and later enacted, it reflected the same notion of states' rights and individual rights, as the Articles, and the last claimant on the rights list was the federal government in Washington D.C. The founders abhorred the notion of a strong central government such as a monarchy—like that of England's George III. Can we blame them. Many today have similar sympathies, as shown during the Obama presidency.

Under the Articles of Confederation, each of the states retained its "sovereignty, freedom, and independence." The preamble of the US Constitution drafted in 1787 and ratified later by the individual states one at a time, sets its purpose as "in order to form a more perfect *union*." Union of course refers to the united part of the United States.

The founders of our government recognized that there were flaws in the Articles of Confederation that would more easily permit a tyranny to take place. And, so their best, "more perfect" work, the Constitution, a 2.0 on the Articles of Confederation in Microsoft - speak, was their way of correcting those flaws and assuring the notion of a constitutional representative democracy (aka, a Republic) for the United States.

There was a permanent institution called the Congress formed in the Articles as a national legislature comprised of representatives of the states. The Congress was responsible for conducting foreign affairs, declaring war or peace, maintaining an army and navy and a variety of other lesser functions.

The Articles did not call for the separation of powers with an executive, legislative, and judicial branch. The Articles did not permit the delegates to collect taxes, regulate interstate commerce and enforce laws. These were the people's rights, aka, the State's rights.

Under the Articles of Confederation these important functions could only be performed by the central government if the states agreed, and only for as long as the states agreed.

Though the Articles had shortcomings, this historical and functional document provided the guidelines for the United States government and it was the only real law of the land until the Constitution was adopted and ratified.

Eventually, the shortcomings were addressed and this lead to the U.S. Constitution. The beauty of the Articles of Confederation was that it provided a workable framework during those years in which the 13 states were struggling to achieve their independent status from being one-time colonies of England.

Considering that the Constitution itself is under fire today by those who would like it constructed in ways that were not intended by the Founding Fathers, from November 15, 1777, when adopted by the Congress, the Articles of Confederation did its job to keep the Country in good stead. Nothing in life worth having is easy.

On March1, 1781, two years before the end of the War, the Articles became operational when the last of the thirteen states signed the document. The next major historical happening in the formation of our government was the work of the framers to create the US Constitution.

Chapter 14 Why did the Confederation Fail?

The Articles were simply not good enough for America!

The Articles of Confederation, the direct predecessor of the Constitution had many great features but it was far from perfect. If the US was an island and would never face enemies, it would not have been as bad a structure but in reality, it was not the body of law that would keep America safe and prosperous. And, so it needed to be amended to make it work for the good of the country.

The Confederation formed by the Articles brought no transformation of the government to satisfy the needs of a growing country. It did place on a legal foundation a structure that unfortunately needed rebuilding throughout. The main, and fatal, character of the government under the Articles is listed in Article II, "Each state retains its sovereignty, freedom, and independence, and every Power, Jurisdiction and right, which is not by this confederation expressly delegated to the United States." It was therefore a "league of friendship," with no teeth for enforcement.

Congress was the unique organ in which "each state shall have one vote." The vote of nine States in Congress was necessary to get anything done. The Articles contained many wise details, which later were written into the Constitution; but this imperfect arrangement gave Congress no control and no power to raise money. A broke country, a weak country be!

The US central government could only make requisitions on the states (as it had done during the war), and then hope and pray that the states would give up the purse as requested. States were too autonomous and did not like giving the federal government any money and so they rarely did, and thus the central governing capability of the country was impaired and to be honest, it was categorically ineffective. With a treasury $20 trillion out of balance today, there is again a case to be made for states' rights. Once the knaves get to Washington, they think they are playing with monopoly money.

The Congress was given control over foreign affairs but was given no means of making the states obey even the treaty requirements, or provide for the payment of the foreign debt. It was a government of responsibility without power. To foreign nations it was the united-states but to the states, it was merely what they chose to make it as the states held all the cards. Its dealing with the people was through States and not vice versa. It was tough to move this huge country into any action and it became even more difficult as the states grew.

During the Revolutionary War, our war of independence, most of the States had adopted constitutions of their own. These provided for governments in separate departments—executive, legislative, and judicial—with bills of rights to protect the citizens especially from such evils as had caused the revolt against British control. They were based on the practices of colonial times and the current theories of government; and they gave control through the elective franchise over the lower house of legislature in all cases, as had been the rule of the colonies.

In the state governments that came about, there was usually an upper house, but the character of its election varied. The governor was chosen by the legislature. In only five cases, the four New England States and New York, was there a legislature with a chief executive elected by the people. The Articles of Confederation were, however, a thing apart from this movement, a concession to necessity rather than an inherent element of American polity. It is tough to form a government but the founders, who were truly honorable men, went about the process honorably. Only Benedict Arnold is noted as a traitor in the major history books.

Though it was successful in prosecuting the war, mainly because of the raw intelligence, cunning, and persistence of George Washington, it is small wonder that the Confederation was not a success. Congress recognized at once the financial need; but several efforts to get the States to amend the Articles, by adding the right to levy import duties, failed through lack of unanimous authorization. The Articles actually inhibited their being changed for the better.

Once the war ended, there was a collapse of moral fiber that seems always to follow a great clash of arms. Interest in the union steadily waned. States began to behave as independent countries. It became increasingly difficult to secure a quorum of attendance in Congress, and when there was a sufficiency of states represented, important measures were often blocked by the need to have nine state votes.

The time following the war was a period of economic distress. It was also a time of experimentation, of learning a hard lesson in government that would be remembered. The Continental Congress and Articles of Confederation not only remained a symbol of union; they also prepared the way for a better national government and left on hand agencies of government in good working order and various substantial acts of legislation.

Among these were the ordinance for the government of the Northwest Territory, and that for the public-land survey. Yet, the tone was set that either the Confederation needed major improvement; or a new and more perfect form of government needed to be established. Plans were drawn up for both.

Chapter 15 The Road from the Confederation to the Constitution

The Virginia Plan

On May 29, 1787, the Constitutional Convention, as convened for the purpose of improving the government, was ready to begin business. President Randolph "opened the main business" by introducing the "Virginia Plan." The intent was to either make the Articles of Confederation work for the new nation as a whole or to scrap them.

The Virginia Plan suggested scrapping most of the Articles and borrowing from the documentation in the Articles to fill in missing pieces of the Virginia Plan. Could this work or would it look like Virginia's plan for a central government. a

This plan, drafted by Madison, a patriot and founder, had been submitted by him in outline to George Washington on April 16, 1787, and it was later worked up in preliminary meetings of the Virginia delegation of seven members. What did it suggest the nation do? It provided for apportioned representation, a legislature of two houses, the lower house (House) elected by the people, the upper one (Senate) was to have representatives (Senators) elected by the legislatures of the states.

The legislature was to have all the legislative powers of the Continental Congress, and also "to legislate in all cases to which the separate States are incompetent, or in which the harmony of the United States may be interrupted by the exercise of individual Legislation; to negate all laws passed by the several States, contravening in the opinion of the National Legislature the articles of Union; and to call forth the force of the Union against any member of the Union failing to fulfill its duty under the articles thereof."

"There was to be a national executive [President] and a national judiciary, with a council of revision formed out of them, which needed to have a conditional veto on national legislation and also on the national legislature's shutting down any State acts. The central power was to guarantee a republican [not Republican Party) form of government and its territory to each State. Provisions for the admission of new States were included, and provisions for amendment without the assent of the National Legislature were part of the proposal."

Also, State officers were to be "bound by oath to support the articles of Union." This was the foundation for what was to become the Constitution of the United States. For its form, it went back to practices of colonial and state governments; for its powers to the lessons of wartime and later experiences.

It gave the central government coercive power over the State governments, while it guaranteed the continued existence of state governments. Since it made no provision for operation through the state governments, it contained the idea of direct action on the people, and the great "law of the land" principle was foreshadowed.

This was far more than a mere amendment of the Articles of Confederation and entirely contrary to the instructions given the delegates from Delaware. It was a large-State proposal.

Charles Pinckney also introduced a plan, the text of which is difficult to find in the archives, but probable extracts and an outline exist. Its general character was similar to the Virginia plan and its influence upon the final draft seems to have been considerable. FYI Pinckney had been the 37th Governor of South Carolina, a Senator and a member of the House of Representatives. He was a patriotic man worth listening to.

The next thirteen meetings were in committee of the whole upon the Virginia plan. To enforce the idea of this plan three resolutions, urged by Gouverneur Morris, were introduced declaring that a federal (that is, confederate) union of individual sovereigns was not sufficient; that a "national Government ought to be established consisting of a supreme Legislative, Executive, & Judiciary."

BTW, Governor Morris was quite a patriot. He was an American statesman, a Founding Father of the United States, and a signatory to the Articles of Confederation and the United States Constitution.

The report which the committee of the whole made to the convention on June 13 was a development of the Virginia plan, with changes that gave the election of the upper house of the national legislature to the State legislatures; made the executive consist of a single individual, and gave him alone the provisional veto; and added a resolution for the ratification of the new Constitution by State conventions. Nobody was looking for a return to the law of tyranny by English dictators or pro-English Americans.

The Paterson Plan

During this period with the Articles forming the legitimacy of the US government, the rights of Americans were hanging in the balance. Meanwhile a number of the constitutional convention delegates (aka deputies) feared a strong central government. They had reason to fear it but without it they might have more to fear. How about a retake by England or a conquest by another global power wanting to attack an apparently weak nation?

Their major concern was with preserving the power of the States. To this end, they devised an alternative plan, which was introduced by Paterson of New Jersey on June 15, 1787.

This merely added to the Articles, the power for Congress to have the right to levy an impost and to regulate foreign and interstate commerce. It also authorized a plural executive and a federal judiciary. It made the acts of Congress and the treaties with foreign powers "the supreme law of the respective States so far forth as those Acts or Treaties shall relate to the said States or their Citizens," and it bound the judiciary of the States to proper observance. It also gave the national executive the right to call forth the power of the States to compel obedience by the States to such acts or treaties.

In essence, this plan left the character of Congress unchanged, with an equal State vote and choice of delegates by the State legislatures; it adopted the separation of national powers; and specified the supremacy of the Union within its sphere. There were thus concessions to the recognized need for a more efficient government, but they did not go very far. They merely patched up the old Articles; and not so well to heal them.

From this, a compromise

As human beings from today might suspect, there was always a battle between the large and small states with the powerful states wanting to more-say in the national government. To avoid a convention ending result, and no improvements to the government, the Connecticut deputies urged adoption of what was known as a Great Compromise.

As hard as it may be to believe, out of the great conflict, which threatened to disrupt the convention, on July 16, 1787, emerged the adoption of this Great Compromise.

This gave representation based on population in the lower house, with the exclusive power to originate money bills in that House; but in the upper house an equal State vote. The special financial power of the lower house was also a provision in some of the state constitutions; but it was later practically nullified by giving the US Senate the right of unrestricted amendment.

During the discussion of this, a major division between the northern and southern states developed, due to the latter's demand to include their slave population in the delegate count.

As tough as it is for any of us to stomach now, remember slavery was legal back then. Importation of slaves remained legal for about thirty more years. As such, a big part of the compromise was to have slaves count towards the representation tally.

The compromise dictated that three-fifths of the slaves should be counted as inhabitants. Those believing everything about America's founding was bad would like you to believe that Americans thought slaves were only 60% human. Nothing could have been and is further from the truth. There were both white and black slaves.

This compromise, together with the election of the Senate by the State legislatures (aka the people in general), did much to quiet the apprehension of the small-state party; but it was not a victory for those who wished to preserve the principles of the Articles of Confederation. When later each senator was given a separate vote, the idea of State representation in the upper house was weakened but it was a better notion than thirteen separate states warring against each other.

This compromise made it evident that sectional questions as well as those involving state's rights were to be met. This evidence was prophetic of future trouble as solutions were not determined but the concord for a method of united states governance had been achieved, Yes, over time, it needed to be improved.

Law of the Land

The next important question was that of national control over state laws and actions. The delegates recognized its need but they had a problem with the notion of a direct veto and the idea of military enforcement of obedience was objectionable.

The plan noted above, as introduced by Paterson on June 15, 1787, suggested the remedy, which was adopted unanimously on July 17, 1787. This made the laws and treaties of the national government the supreme law, to which the state judiciaries were bound in their decisions.

Later the Constitution itself was added to the laws and treaties and the "supreme law of the states" was made the "Supreme law of the land," which change might be considered as emphasizing the origin of the Constitution as the work of the whole-of the people-and not just of the states.

This great "Law of the Land" clause has been called the linchpin of the Constitution, since it effectively binds the parts into the whole. It has always been the chief basis upon which the courts have passed on the constitutionality of legislation, whether state or national. It embodies the principle of direct action by the national government upon the inhabitants, for the enactments of the Congress, the people's representatives, are laws directly binding upon the people themselves.

The New Government

The league of states embodied in the Articles of Confederation was made by the states with minimal adherence to the notion of a central power. The Constitution was made by the People. The first three words of the Constitution— "We the People"—declare by what authority the United States of America was created and is to be ruled.

Having won their liberty and independence by force of arms, and having experienced distress and danger because of an imperfect union, the people finally succeeded in forming the more perfect Union which is ordained and established by the Constitution.

The Constitution is a direct emanation from the people. It not only prescribes the kind of government, which shall hold the states and the people together, but it limits and defines the powers of the government itself. Neither the United States Government nor the states can modify, enlarge, or restrict their own powers.

They depend for their existence upon the people, who reserve the right as set forth in the Declaration of Independence, to alter or abolish their government. Until the people decide otherwise, the United States is, in the noble phrase of Chief Justice Chase, "an indissoluble Union of indestructible States."

Many states today as in the 1860's with the secession and slavery issues, are upset at the lawlessness of the government, and are talking about the viability of secession, just like the prior president's executive orders were lawless, secession would also be lawless. However, if a president is lawless, and Congress remains indifferent and permits the lawlessness, one would think that implicitly the states would be authorized to secede from a lawless government that itself does not adhere to the Constitution. That sure is a mouthful!

Short of dissolving the entire government, a right which the people have possessed since they declared independence from England, secession may be a preferred method in a lawless land. This battle has yet to be fought but we are approaching a time in which the red and the blue states may very well choose to be on separate sides of two new governments. Those who support the President in 2017, carry guns that they hope to never use but the popular press seems to believe that groups like Antifa trump the regular people. Will at some time we hear a new shot heard round the world?

The movement has quieted down now with Trump in Office but the secession movement was for real. In January 2013, the "secession petitions filed by residents of Texas, Louisiana, Alabama and five other states, as well as one counterpetition seeking the deportation of everyone who signed a secession petition," received an official response from White House Office of Public Engagement director Jon Carson.

Carson rejected the secession notion, writing that open debate was positive for democracy but that the founders had established a "perpetual union" and that the Supreme Court ruled in Texas v. White (1869) that individual states had no right to secede. Of course, if there were a Constitutional Amendment, all bets are off.

If all was perfect, the union would be indissoluble by the Constitution, which also provides for the indestructibility of the states by guaranteeing to each State a republican form of government and equal suffrage in the Senate. Nobody today can say that government is operating as intended by the founders.

Ironically, the model for major parts of our government including the major structural document—The Constitution—came from studying the British model. Yet, England has no written constitution. Its constitution or fundamental law is whatever Parliament says it is.

Hard as it may be to believe, Britain has no codified constitution but an unwritten one formed of Acts of Parliament, court judgments and conventions. Therefore, the judges of England enforce the laws of Parliament without any question as to their constitutionality.

In a republic such as the US, with a written constitution creating a government with limited powers, a nation must have some means of determining if laws are in accord with the basic principles set forth by the constitution.

The liberties enjoyed by Englishmen were wrested from the Crown. The American colonists claimed these liberties as their inheritance, and won by force of arms, the final right to them and to further ones which had been fostered by the conditions of the colonial governments.

"The government of the United States is not a concession to the people from someone higher up. It is the creation and the creature of the people themselves, as absolute sovereigns."

Who could have said this any better than Sol Bloom, the author of the 1937 best seller during the time of the Constitution's Sesquicentennial (150th anniversary)—"The Story of the Constitution." Let's Go Publish!, the publisher of this book, has re-mastered Sol Bloom's epoch, and it is available for purchase at www.amazon.com/author/brianwkelly.

Chapter 16 The US Constitution

Introduction to the Constitution

The founders were mainly pleased with the Constitution as a more perfect union than the Articles of Confederation. Those who wrote the Articles of Confederation admitted its imperfections not too long after its ratification. It was an imperfect constitution for the newly formed union but far better than having no law of the land.

The Congress read the Letters of Delegates to Congress, which contained drafts of the Articles of Confederation, written by Josiah Bartlett and John Dickinson from late June 1776. Both Bartlett and Dickinson were members of the committee tasked with writing the draft of the Articles of Confederation.

Let's review the adoption of the Articles of Confederation before we move directly to the Constitution. After fine tuning the drafts presented in the Letters, The Continental Congress adopted the Articles of Confederation, the first constitution of the United States, on November 15, 1777.

However, ratification of the Articles of Confederation by all thirteen states did not occur until March 1, 1781. The Articles created a loose confederation of sovereign states and a weak central government, leaving most of the power with the state governments. The need for a stronger Federal government soon became apparent and eventually led to the Constitutional Convention in 1787. The present United States Constitution replaced the Articles of Confederation on March 4, 1789.

To put the Constitution in proper perspective, we can ask ourselves if it would have been possible for Bill Gates to have introduced Windows 10 in 1985 rather than Windows 1.0? That answer is a clear no.

Mr. Gates and Microsoft needed to go through all of the versions from Windows 1.0 to Windows 10 to learn what was needed in Windows 10. This is similar to how The Constitution is a better version of the first law of the land, the Articles of Confederation. Once there is a basis for something, it can be improved. As version 1.0, The Articles were well done but needed improvement. A "more perfect union" was necessary. The Constitution represents version 2.0.

The additional features in the Constitution over the Articles of Confederation are substantial. In many ways, it was like going from Windows 1.0 to Windows 98. Then, of course the Bill of Rights was like moving to Windows NT from 98. Now, add in the 17 other constitutional amendments, each a minor update to the Constitution, and we can ask ourselves in Microsoft parlance, "What version of the Constitution are we running today?

As an aside, besides the powers of government being separated, which items gave the government a higher probability for tyranny? George Washington described the biggest problem with the Articles of Confederation in just two words, "no money."

Under the Articles, the Federal government relied on the states for funding. Without the Constitution, America might really be the name of a large land mass with 48 countries, and two not so contiguous countries--Hawaii and Alaska. A country with no money could not survive over the long haul.

The barebones Constitution itself was far more perfect than the Articles of Confederation, just like Windows 98 was far more perfect than Windows 1.0. Microsoft could not immediately go to Windows 10 because nobody knew how any of the other previous versions would behave or be accepted, and all the subsequent iterations of Windows occurred from its use over time, and its technological successes and failings. So, with the Constitution! Besides, for Microsoft, substantially less powerful hardware could run Windows 1.0 fine but would have a coughing spell trying to boot Windows 10.

In many ways, our country grew the same way—in stages. The phrase "a more perfect union," in the Preamble of the Constitution notes the

imperfections in a prior version and it introduces the rationale for the drawing of the *Constitution* from the *Articles of Confederation.*
We know from reading the prior chapters that the imperfect document was *The Articles of Confederation*. Bill Gates knew that the prior document to Windows was the last version of DOS without the Windows GUI. He knew he could make it better after he visited Xerox's Palo Alto Research Center and learned about GUI in the mid 1970's.

The U.S. Constitution (and its subsequent 27 amendments) mimics the idea of having a v3.1, V4.1.x, and V5.x.3. It has survived for over well over two-hundred years without many changes. This notion of a basis document and then perfections in subsequent versions testifies to the eventual almost perfection of the Constitution.

Like Windows, it went through multiple iterations to get to The Constitution. Back in 1787, it was built to be the basis of the constitutional representative democracy (Republic) of the United States. If he were alive at the time, even Bill Gates would have approved.

From the National Archives:

http://www.archives.gov/national-archives-experience/charters/constitution.html

I like how this text from the national archives reads—so instead of trying to rephrase this, I have included it below to explain the purpose of the work behind the Constitution. We have heard this before in this book, and so it should ring quite familiar.

> *"The Federal Convention convened in the State House (Independence Hall) in Philadelphia on May 14, 1787, to revise the Articles of Confederation. Because the delegations from only two states were at first present, the members adjourned from day to day until a quorum of seven states was obtained on May 25. [I would bet the adjournments took the quorum-less participants to Philadelphia's historic City Tavern, a fine place even today to libate.] Through discussion and debate it became clear by mid-June that, rather than amend the existing Articles, the Convention would draft an entirely new frame of government.*

The City Tavern, Philadelphia, PA

Best entrance view. Operating since 1773.

"All through the summer, in closed sessions, the delegates debated, and redrafted the articles of the new Constitution. Among the chief points at issue were how much power to allow the central government, how many representatives in Congress to allow each state, and how these representatives should be elected--directly by the people or by the state legislators. The work of many minds, the Constitution stands as a model of cooperative statesmanship and the art of compromise."

The Law of the Land

As noted previously, since 1787, the Constitution of the United States has comprised the primary law of the U.S. Federal Government. In simple terms, it is the law of the land, and all other laws must conform to the statutes contained within this original document and its amendments, from the Bill of Rights to Amendment # 27.

This law also describes the three chief branches of the Federal Government and their jurisdictions as well as the separation of the powers. It also gives the nation the ability to levy taxes, though an income tax was not permitted in the Constitution on people or corporations. Let's take a break and look more closely at the income tax amendment. We'll be back soon to continue our discussion.

Ironically, and quite smartly, there was no income tax provision in The Constitution. The founders did not want a personal or corporate income tax mainly because it might be apportioned so that certain states paid more than others to the central government.

The people in the early twentieth century for their own reasons voted to ratify the Sixteenth amendment to the Constitution. This gave the Congress the right to tax them and US, and corporations at a personal level. Dum, Dumm, Dummm, and Dummmer must have been the lawyers representing the people in the campaign for passage of this terrible amendment. In the passage of this law, there was both chicanery and a lot more irony.

As hard as it may be to believe, the Sixteenth Amendment, which gave the American people the misery of confiscatory income taxes, was a trick. It never was supposed to have passed. Good people representing good people would never have permitted it.

It was introduced by the Republicans as part of a political scheme to fake-out the Democrats from a tax increase bill that would have passed but could never have been enforced because it would be unconstitutional. But, the Republican trick backfired.

As previously noted, the Founding Fathers had rejected income taxes (as well as any other direct taxes) in the Constitution unless they were apportioned to each state according to population.

The politicians in the US Senate in the early 1900s passed a bill to institute the Sixteenth Amendment permitting such direct taxation in violation of the founders' intentions. They wanted more largesse to distribute by getting more dollars in the treasury from taxpayers to assure their elections. It was their first grab at redistribution of income.

The people of course would have to ratify such an amendment if it passed Congress. It surprisingly passed unanimously 77-0 in the Senate! The House also approved it by another large margin, 318-14. Nobody was thinking, including the people in the states!

It was then sent to the states for ratification. State after state ratified this "soak the rich" amendment, thinking it would not affect them until it went into full force and effect on February 12, 1913. The people voted to tax the rich but just about everybody has been taxed ever since. You can never outfox a foxy politician. Democratic President Wilson was the best at politics and communism and progressivism, but he was not a very good leader in other ways.

In the Economic Policy Journal in April 2012, David, a blogger, called it right with his opinion of many Americans. His explanation, which is quoted below is that Americans would not vote for somebody, even Ron Paul who they truly believe would eliminate the income tax on everybody, because they think the rich should pay all the taxes and they should pay none. David sees it as a matter of class envy and offers a bleak outlook on the chances of it getting better until people wake up. Let's not be David, please. See what he has to say:

"Americans are envious and covetous of the wealth of others. They don't want freedom. They like a government that will do things to them, so long as the resulting chains appear to be gold plated. They like politicians that stir up class envy. Humans by nature are slaves. They don't yearn to be free, responsible, independent people. Until this wholly selfish and self-centered people awaken from their slumber; and learn to hate their slavery to government, until the iron of their chains eats into their soul, things are going to get worse."

The fact that Americans are beginning to get upset is a good sign. More and more people, like you, the reader, will be looking to learn about their rights and then I predict they will come after government with a vengeance. The times when politicians could survive despite their malfeasance in office are about to end because the people are about to end it. Thank you for reading this book.

I like to repeat to make a point. The fact that good citizens such as you are reading a book about the Bill of Rights is another good sign. I think this will all turn around with the help of some good leaders. That means we Americans must do our best to kick every federal politician (representative) out of office and replace them with good people as soon as we can. Then we take our battle to the state capitals, and then the cities. Finally, America will be run by the people again.

Back to the Constitution

In addition to permitting all but direct taxation, The Constitution lays out the basic rights of citizens of the United States. The Constitution of the United States is the oldest federal constitution in existence in the world, and it was framed by a convention of delegates from twelve of the thirteen original states in Philadelphia in May 1787.

The Constitution is the landmark legal document of the United States and all other laws are tested against its specifications. Many other constitutions, such as the Constitution of Mexico, for example are based on this work.

The text of the entire Constitution is available for free on the Internet as well as hardcopy books for sale in bookstores. Your author's best seller Taxation Without Representation includes Appendices with all of the founding documents mentioned in this book.

The Bill of Rights (first ten amendments) and the other 17 amendments are described in detail in subsequent chapters. There are also a number of Amendments that were submitted but did not pass. This would make interesting reading on the Internet.

The Constitution is a free document for anybody to record and retransmit in any form. It is over two hundred twenty-five years old. It makes America, America.

Summary of the US Constitution

Explanation / Summary of Article I of the US Constitution:

Article I: The Legislative Branch consists of 10 sections and defines:

1. All Legislative powers,
2. Composition of the House of Representatives,
3. Composition of the Senate
4. Holding Elections,
5. Congress sets its own rules by House,
6. Compensation for Senators,
7. Revenue Bills originate in House,
8. Congress can lay and collect taxes,
9. States' rights and taxes,
10. State treaties.

Note: Article I, Section 9, Clause 8 of the Constitution is of particular interest to this writer.

For your convenience, this is provided below:

> ***Section 9 Clause 8:*** *No Title of Nobility shall be granted by the United States: And no Person holding any Office of Profit or Trust under them, shall, without the Consent of the Congress, accept of any present, Emolument, Office, or Title, of any kind whatever, from any King, Prince, or foreign State.*

Article II: The Executive Branch: Consists of 4 sections and defines:

(1) Executive Power and President, (2) President as Commander in Chief, (3) State of the Union & Information Requirements, (4) Rules of Executive Branch impeachment

Article III: The Judicial Branch: Consists of 3 sections and defines:

(1) Judicial Power, (2) Laws and Trial by Jury, (3) Treason

Article IV: Relations Between States: Consists of 4 sections and defines:

(1) Faith and Credit of State Laws, (2) Privileges apply to all in all states, (3) New States May be Admitted to the Union, (4) Federal guarantee to defend states.

Article V: The Amendment Process: Consists of 1 section and defines the amendment process for adding / deleting to/from the Constitution.

Article VI: General Provisions, Supremacy of the Constitution: Consists of 1 section and defines the debt process and the requirement to support the Constitution

Article VII: Ratification Process: Consists of 1 section and it outlines the process for ratifying the Constitution.

End of Constitution summary. The full text of the US Constitution is available for free on the Internet.

Chapter 17 Rights Must Be Earned. None Are Given Freely!

Patriots were tough; fought for their rights & would not be pushed around

Americans have believed in their rights and freedoms and liberties for many years—long before the Constitution. In fact, the notion of American rights goes far back into Colonial America when British subjects outnumbered all other immigrants and were under British dominion. These colonists brought with them the traditions of British' rights, liberties, and immunities, British laws and customs, and the English language to boot.

The notion of privileges and immunities is not something that we hear about every day or something we use in everyday language. Privileges and immunities for our purposes in this book are concepts contained in the U.S. Constitution that place the citizens of each state on an equal basis with citizens of all other states in respect to advantages resulting from citizenship in those states and citizenship in the United States.

The privileges and immunities of which we speak are protected under Article IV of the Constitution and they include the right to receive protection from state government; the right to acquire and possess all kinds of property; the right to travel through or reside in any state for purposes of trade, agriculture, or professional endeavors; the right to claim the benefit of the writ of Habeas Corpus; the right to sue and defend actions in court; and the right to receive the same tax treatment as that of the citizens of the taxing state. As you will see, these rights are not the same exact rights that we find in the Bill of Rights.

Most countries from time immemorial have been run by absolutists and dictators. An absolute monarch for example, is one who wields unrestricted political and executive power over the sovereign state and its people. Over time, in more enlightened countries such as England, the people have been able to bargain for more rights from the government. But, this is not the case in most absolutist countries.

During the 1700s, for example, the England that lorded over the colonists was governed under a mixed "semi-constitution," made up of the monarch, the House of Lords and the House of Commons. These two houses were collectively known as Parliament. This type of government in the 1700s for England was the result of events that occurred in the previous century, when King Charles I was executed and England briefly became a republic.

Eventually the monarchy was restored in 1660. Charles II became king, but the new parliament held many more powers than had been the case during Charles I's reign. In other words, the English people gained additional rights.

And, so we can say that it was centuries of struggle that had won for Englishmen many guarantees of rights, liberties, and immunities. English common law was fairly established when the colonies were begun. Some rights and immunities, which had been enjoyed from time immemorial by the English, were reduced to writing in the Magna Charta, which was squeezed out of King John by the barons of England at Runnymede way back in 1215. Rights are not something foreign to the English people.

Other individual rights in England were formally guaranteed in writing, notably the Bill of Rights under William and Mary in 1689. The system of "constitutional government" safeguarded by a parliament elected by the people was well established when the first colonial charter was granted.

It helps to note that the liberties and rights of Britons were concessions from kings who ruled as by divine right and who originally possessed all authority. These concessions, and continual concessions over time, underlie the monarchical system to this day.

Colonial Americans wanted English rights

The colonies, beginning with Virginia and New England, were settled under charters granted by the King of England. These grants made large reservations of royal privilege and relatively small concessions to the emigrants. Broadly speaking, the colonists did not at first enjoy civil and political liberties as they were known in England.

Protests against denial of privileges enjoyed by British freemen were made in Virginia as early as 1612. Gradually the colonies were given larger powers of government, always provided that colonial laws should be in conformity to the laws of England and that allegiance to the Crown should be acknowledged.

The colonial period of the people who became Americans technically can be defined as from 1492 to 1788, which was the year in which the US Constitution was ratified. It therefore established the USA as we now know it. The period of English dominance in the Colonies began much later than 1492, and lasted about 170 years. The colonists therefore had abundant experience during this period in various forms of government under British authority, and they well knew a right from a prohibition.

In some respects, eventually the colonists achieved substantial home rule and they enjoyed many individual liberties equals to those enjoyed by the English in England. But in matters of trade, the British government persisted in sacrificing the rights of the colonies to the advantage of Britain. This situation developed endless friction, complaint, and evasion of the British regulations. Americans, from England, or from elsewhere, resented the use of their success to fund the Crown for a perception of no value received.

When the colonists revolted against England, it was not as much because they had no rights as that they were treated as step-children, and a source of booty for England. The colonists were enraged at the treatment and would sacrifice life and limb to gain back their perception of freedom. As we all know, and thank the Lord for providing, America prevailed in the Revolution and eventually drafted its own Constitution.

As of 2017, only twenty-seven amendments have been attached to the Constitution. We call the first ten of these amendments, the Bill of Rights. As previously discussed in this book, the Bill of Rights did not come without controversy. However, unlike today's me-first politicians, the founders cared enough to work to make sure they got the best deal for Americans for all time to come.

The conventions of several States consented to ratify the Constitution only after they became satisfied that the Bill of Rights would be made an important part of it. Memorializing this achievement, many are aware that on March 18, 1936, in an eloquent address to the United States Senate, dealing specifically with the fourth and fifth amendments, Senator Ashurst of Arizona gave a vivid picture of the genesis of the Bill of Rights.

This is a fitting introduction for a detailed discussion of The Bill of Rights. This speech has been is extracted from *Sol Bloom's … Epoch Story of the Constitution* a work edited by your author and published by Let's Go Publish! —available online at www.amazon.com/author/brianwkelly.

Referring to the ancient right expressed in the phrase, "Every man's house is his castle," Mr. Ashurst said:

"A gentleman calling upon me once asked, 'Did you ever read Lord Coke's famous maxim in Semayne's case?' to wit, 'The house of every one is to him as his castle and fortress, as well for his defense against injury and violence as for his repose.' I said, 'I am familiar with Coke, but that was law 1,000 years before my Lord Coke adorned the bench. ' "

Senator Ashurst added:

"The makers of our Federal Constitution and the framers of the first 10 amendments were never tired of quoting the immortal words of the elder Pitt, used in his speech on The Excise:

'The poorest man may in his cottage bid defiance to all the force of the Crown. It may be frail; its roof may shake; the wind may blow through it; the storms may enter; the rain may enter-but the King of

England cannot enter. All his forces dare not cross the threshold of the ruined tenement.'

Virginia's Struggles

"When the ratification of the Federal Constitution was pending before the Virginia convention, called to pass upon that momentous question, Virginia was a pivotal State—a diamond pivot—on which mighty events turned.

Patrick Henry, whom Lord Byron said was 'the forest-born Demosthenes who shook the Phillip of the seas,' was a delegate to the Virginia convention; and although the proposed Federal Constitution had come forth with the sanction of the revered name of General Washington and therefore justly carried with it the vast prestige which the name of Washington could not fail to attach to any proposition, Patrick Henry did not approve the Constitution and, to use his own expression, he was 'most awfully alarmed,' as he considered the document to be threatening to the liberties of his country—amongst other reasons because it lacked a bill of rights—and Mr. Henry challenged the view of Mr. James Madison, he of the superb intellect; Mr. Henry challenged the Wythes, the Pendletons, and the Innesses, and that splendid galaxy of scholars and statesmen who enriched the annals not only of Virginia but all America; and he demanded to know why a Bill of Rights, guaranteeing the privileges and immunities of the citizen, had been omitted from the Federal Constitution."

Bravo Patrick Henry! We all know that this fine American was surely a patriot! Great people take a toll, most often positive, on the efforts of the unsure. Patrick Henry was as sure of his convictions and his words as those who fought him were sure of theirs. The opposition could not figure out why Henry was wrong, and consequently, since it was all good people in the debate, giving in was not so hard—even for other great patriots among the founders.

The Virginia State convention, after a prolonged debate, was able to ratify the Federal Constitution by a majority of only 10 votes, so ably did Patrick Henry argue against it because it did not contain the Bill of Rights, which English liberty had affirmed for centuries.

James Madison pledged his word that at the earliest opportunity he would use his energy toward placing into the Federal Constitution the requisite amendments guaranteeing the citizens' rights, privileges, and immunities, and as soon as the Virginia convention had finished the work of ratification it adopted resolutions expressing its desire for the Bill of Rights, as demanded by Patrick Henry. Madison was true to his word.

These resolutions were forwarded to the governors of the various states, and as far as men could be bound in faith and honor, as far as men could be bound in statesmanship and in politics, the amendments guaranteeing the citizen's individual rights and his liberties were by common consent agreed to, and it was generally understood that these amendments would be proposed to the states by the First Congress.

The Constitution therefore was ratified first without the Bill of Rights. It was not possible to amend the Constitution as prescribed in the Constitution without first there being a Constitution. The Constitution established the Congress and the presidency, and the Courts system.

The first bill to be considered by the First Congress under the Constitution was quite naturally a bill to raise revenue to pay the many expenses of the government which had already incurred. But, as expected, the next had to do with rights! On July 21, 1789, James Madison, who was a Member of the House, arose and asked the House 'to indulge him in further consideration of amendments to the Constitution.'

Madison pointed out that the faith and honor of Congress were pledged; that the faith and honor of public men everywhere were pledged to amendments securing to the citizens such guaranties as were comprehended within the first ratified 10 amendments.

"The Bill of Rights amendments were then proposed to the States, including of course the fourth and fifth, and were ratified within 2 years and 3 months. Thereafter, as far as Americans are concerned, and as far as the Constitution itself is concerned, they were and are a part and parcel of the original Constitution, as much so as if they were signed on the 17th of September 1787, when the main instrument itself was signed."

Chapter 18 The First Ten Restrictions on Central Government Power

The Bill of Rights protects the people

The ten amendments constituting the Bill of Rights are restrictions upon national power. As we see today in America, the elusive notion of the people possessing all power on all issues regarding powers not granted specifically to the Federal Government, falls apart when a president such as the past president simply does not buy that argument. Then, with a corrupt press in his tank, he subtly convinces half of the American people that he is above the law—and that it is perceived by the press and an apparent majority as OK! That, my dear readers, is exactly why some people write books about rights.

The rights and immunities enumerated in the Bill of Rights were already in existence with the ratification of the Constitution but they were not explicit. The people had all their rights and liberties after the war even before they created the Constitution. The Constitution was established to assure these rights, among other purposes, to make the people's liberties secure against oppression by the government, which they were in the process of setting up.

The Bill of Rights was created to make the people more comfortable with the notion that the government would be controlled, by the people, and would operate for the people, and be operated of the people. Let's now take a quick ride through the essence of each of the first ten rights outlined in the Bill of Rights. Americans need every one of these amendments regardless of executive orders to the contrary.

I.

The First Amendment, related to religion, free speech, right of assembly and petition, debars Congress from establishing a religion or prohibiting free exercise of religion, or abridging the freedom of speech or of the press, or the right of the people peaceably to assemble and to petition the Government for a redress of grievances.

Efforts to check the evil practices of lobbying for most of the 20th century and beyond have been checked when they sought to abridge the right of petition; but freedom of speech and of the press does not permit the publication of libels, blasphemous or other indecent articles, or other publications injurious to morals or private reputation.

A publisher is subject to punishment for contempt if his articles tend to obstruct the administration of justice. The right of free speech does not give immunity for every possible use of language.

II.

The Second Amendment confers upon the people the right to bear arms. It also forbids Congress from infringing upon that right.

III.

The Third Amendment protects the people against military intrusion in their homes. In the colonial period, there were times such as by order of the English quartering act, Americans citizens were forced to make their homes available to British soldiers.

IV.

The Fourth Amendment guarantees the security of the people in their persons, houses, papers, and effects against unreasonable searches and seizures. Almost up to the hour of the evolution the American people from subjugated to free, they had suffered from such injuries at the hands of the British government. The people were determined that their own government should not have power to invade their privacy by "writs of assistance," as general search-warrants were called. John Adams, speaking of James Otis' heroic protest against that practice, declared, "The child *independence* was born on that occasion."

V.

The Fifth Amendment protects the citizen against double jeopardy, self-incrimination, deprivation of life, liberty, or property without due process of law, and loss of property taken for public use. Far-reaching decisions by the courts have protected the citizen under these clauses.

VI.

The Sixth Amendment secures the right of trial by jury, and other rights while under criminal trial. The prohibitions are laid upon Congress, and not upon the States.

VII.

The Seventh Amendment guarantees the rights of citizens in civil trials.

VIII.

The Eighth Amendment prohibits excessive bail and fines, and cruel and unusual punishment. The Supreme Court will interfere with the action of state courts if they impose fines which amount to a deprivation of property without due process of law, but will do this under the Fourteenth Amendment.

IX.

The Ninth Amendment provides that the enumeration of certain rights shall not be construed to deny or disparage other rights retained by the people. "This amendment," said the Supreme Court (Livingston v. Moore, 7 Pet. 551) "indicates that the Federal Constitution is but a delegation of powers, which powers, together with the implied powers, constitute all that the Federal Government has or may presume to exercise." The people retain many rights which are not enumerated, and the Government has no power to interfere with these rights.

X.

The Tenth Amendment is vitally important in preserving the powers of the states and the people against encroachment by Congress [and the president]. It retains to the states or the people all powers not delegated to the United States nor prohibited to the States by the Constitution. In observance of this amendment the Supreme Court has halted attempts to invade the powers of the states, notably in the matter of commerce (there have been numerous examples of this in recent years).

The power of the States to regulate matters of internal police applies not only to the health. morals, and safety of the public, but also to whatever promotes the public peace, comfort, and convenience. State laws enacted under this power may be harsh and oppressive without violating the Constitution, but the restrictions of the Fourteenth Amendment apply.

Chapter 19 The Fourteenth Amendment

Fourteenth amendment assures many rights

Since we have referred to the 14th amendment several times in our discussion of the Bill of Rights, let us cover this amendment out of sequence before we proceed with others.

The 14th Amendment to the U.S. Constitution was ratified on July 9, 1868. Along with the 13th and 15th Amendments, these three are collectively known as the Reconstruction amendments. Why? Their origins were the Civil War Period, and they were all ratified during the post-Civil War era. Although the 14th Amendment was originally intended as a solution to protect the rights of the recently freed slaves, it has continued to play a major role in constitutional politics to this day.

14th Amendment & Civil Rights Act of 1866

Of the three Reconstruction amendments, the 14th is the most complicated and the one that has had the more unforeseen effects. Its broad goal was to reinforce the Civil Rights Act of 1866, which ensured that "all persons born in the United States" were citizens and were to be given "full and equal benefit of all laws."

When the Civil Rights Act landed on Democratic President Andrew Johnson's desk, he vetoed it; Congress, in turn, overrode the veto and the measure became law. Johnson, a Tennessee Democrat, had clashed repeatedly with the Republican-controlled Congress. GOP leaders, fearing Johnson and Southern politicians would attempt to redo the Civil War and undo the first Civil Rights Act, then began work on what would become the 14th Amendment.

Ratification & the states

After passing the Congress in June of 1866, the 14th Amendment went to the states for ratification. As a condition for post-war readmittance to the Union, the former Confederate states were required to approve the amendment.

This idea became a point of contention between Congress and Southern leaders. Connecticut was the first state to ratify the 14th Amendment on June 30, 1866. During the next two years, 28 states would ratify the amendment, though not without incident.

For example, legislatures in Ohio and New Jersey both rescinded their states' pro-amendment votes. In the South, both Louisiana and the Carolinas refused initially to ratify the amendment. Nevertheless, the 14th Amendment was declared formally ratified on July 28, 1868.

Sections of the Amendment

There are four specific sections in the 14th Amendment to the U.S. Constitution. It is generally agreed that the first section is the most important.

Section 1 guarantees citizenship to any and all persons born or naturalized in the U.S. It also guarantees all Americans their constitutional rights and denies states the right to limit those rights through legislation. It also ensures a citizen's "life, liberty, or property" will not be denied without due legal process.

Section 2 states that representation to Congress must be determined based on the whole population. In other words, both white and African American had to be counted equally. Prior to this, African American populations were undercounted when apportioning representation. This section also stipulated that all males 21 years or older were guaranteed the right to vote. Women still had not gained suffrage.

Section 3 was designed to prevent former Confederate officers and politicians from holding office. It states that no one may seek federal elected office if they engaged in rebellion against the U.S.

Section 4 addressed the federal debt accrued during the Civil War. It acknowledged that the federal government would honor its debts. It also stipulated that the government would not honor Confederate debts or reimburse slaveholders for wartime losses.

Section 5 essentially affirms Congress' power to enforce the 14th Amendment through legislation.

There are several key clauses

The four clauses of the first section of the 14th Amendment are the most important because they have repeatedly been cited in major Supreme Court cases concerning civil rights, presidential politics and the right to privacy. Nobody looks at these issues as light matters.

The Citizenship Clause states that “All persons born or naturalized in the United States, and subject to the jurisdiction thereof, are citizens of the United States and of the state wherein they reside." This clause played an important role in two Supreme Court cases: Elk v. Wilkins (1884) addressed citizenship rights of Native Americans, while United States v.
Wong Kim Ark (1898) affirmed citizenship of US-born children of legal immigrants.

The Privileges and Immunities Clause states "No state shall make or enforce any law which shall abridge the privileges or immunities of citizens of the United States." In the Slaughter-House Cases (1873), the Supreme Court recognized a difference between a person's rights as a U.S. citizen and their rights under state law. The ruling held that state laws could not impede a person's federal rights. In McDonald v. Chicago (2010), which overturned a Chicago ban on handguns, Justice Clarence Thomas cited this clause in his opinion supporting the ruling.

The Due Process Clause says no state shall "deprive any person of life, liberty, or property, without due process of law." Although this clause was intended to apply to professional contracts and transactions, over time it has become most closely cited in right-to-privacy cases. Notable Supreme Court cases that have turned on this issue include Griswold v. Connecticut (1965), which overturned a Connecticut ban on the sale of contraception; Roe v. Wade (1973), which overturned a Texas ban on abortion and lifted many restrictions on the practice nationwide; and Obergefell v. Hodges (2015), which held that same-sex marriages deserved federal recognition.

The Equal Protection Clause prevents states from denying "to any person within its jurisdiction the equal protection of the laws." The clause has become most closely associated with civil rights cases, particularly for African Americans. In Plessy v. Ferguson (1898) the Supreme Court ruled that Southern states could enforce racial segregation as long as "separate but equal" facilities existed for blacks and whites.

It wouldn't be until Brown v. Board of Education (1954) that the Supreme Court would revisit this opinion, ultimately ruling that separate facilities were, in fact, unconstitutional. This key ruling opened the door for a number of significant civil rights and affirmative action court cases.

Bush v. Gore (2001) also touched on the equal protection clause when a majority of justices ruled that the partial recount of presidential votes in Florida was unconstitutional because it was not being conducted the same way in all contested locations. The decision essentially decided the 2000 presidential election in George W. Bush's favor.

The Legacy of the 14th Amendment

Over time, numerous lawsuits have arisen that have referenced the 14th Amendment. The fact that the amendment uses the word "state" in the *Privileges and Immunities Clause* -- along with interpretation of the

Due Process Clause -- has meant state power and federal power is subject to the Bill of Rights.

Further, the courts have interpreted the word "person" to include corporations. As a result, corporations are also protected by "due process" along with being granted "equal protection."

While there were other clauses in the amendment, none are as significant as these.

Chapter 20 Amendments After The Bill of Rights

Amendments 11 to 27

The good news for all Americans is that the Constitution implicitly grants rights to the people, who are not necessarily properly served by government. But the idea of explicitly noting the people's basic rights to life, a.k.a. the people's rights and the powers of the people is a great idea. The Bill of Rights provides the needed explicit citation of our rights. Amendments 11 to 27 were not seen as major rights issues when the ten amendments in the Bill of Rights were ratified.

All twenty-seven amendments (Including one to ten – the Bill of Rights) together with the un-amended Constitution equals the Constitution of the US

Let's now take a quick ride through the essence of each of the seventeen amendments ratified one at a time after the Bill of Rights. Each of these rights can be seen as a different release of the Constitution, and in few cases, perhaps a different version. If this were Windows, perhaps it would be version 8 or perhaps version 10.

XI.

The Eleventh Amendment exempts a state from suit by a citizen of another state or a foreigner. It does not deprive the Supreme Court of jurisdiction over suits between states. Nor does it prevent suits against individuals holding official positions under a state, to prevent their committing wrong or trespass under sanction of an unconstitutional statute.

XII.

The Twelfth Amendment was declared in effect September 25, 1804, after a deadlock in the election of a President of the United States. Under the original electoral provision, the elector voted "for two Persons," without designating either for President or Vice President. Jefferson and Burr received an equal number of votes in the election of 1800, and 35 ballots were taken in the House of Representatives before the choice fell to Jefferson. The amendment requires electors to vote separately for President and Vice President.

XIII.

The Thirteenth Amendment abolishes slavery. It differs from the first ten amendments in that it restricts the power of the States as well as that of the national government. It removed legal doubt as to the validity of the Emancipation Proclamation.

The drafting of men for military service does not violate this amendment, since a soldier is not a slave; and the contract of a seaman does not violate the spirit of the amendment.

An act of Congress declaring that no distinction should be made between race or color in denying admission to accommodations and privileges in inns, public conveyances and theaters was held unconstitutional [at this time], because denial of these privileges does not subject any person to any form of servitude or fasten upon him any badge of slavery.

XIV.

The Fourteenth Amendment puts beyond doubt that all persons, white or black, whether former slaves or not, born or naturalized, and owing no allegiance to any foreign power, are citizens of the United States and of the state in which they reside.

The states are prohibited from abridging the immunities of citizens, and from depriving any person of life liberty, or property, without due process of law, or denying to any person equal protection of the laws.

A state law fixing the employment of mine workers at eight hours per day does not contravene the amendment. Statutes regulating the manufacture and sale of goods are within the amendment.

The amendment does not add to constitutional privileges and immunities. The right of suffrage is not one of these rights.

But, soon it would be as the nation was able to address its shortcomings.

XV.

The Fifteenth Amendment provides that the right of citizens to vote shall not be denied or abridged on account of race, color, or previous condition of servitude. It does not confer upon any one the right to vote.

The power to determine qualifications of voters is left to the states; but they may not confine the voting right to white persons.

XVI.

The Sixteenth Amendment is the Income Tax Amendment. It gives Congress the power to tax the incomes of the people and corporations from whatever source derived, without apportionment among the several States. This is not an extension of the taxing power, but it removes all occasion for an apportionment among the states of taxes laid upon incomes. The salaries of United States judges are also taxed but cannot be taxed more than the general public, since Article III of the Constitution provides that they shall not be diminished.

With the sixteenth amendment, Congress and the president were permitted to demand all Americans pay for the government through their incomes.

XVII.

The Seventeenth Amendment changes the mode of election of United States senators. Contests in state legislatures over election of senators had caused great dissatisfaction, and it was believed that election by the people would be an improvement.

Some of us still think it is a good idea for the states to elect Senators. In that way, when a Senator chooses to represent the Senator and not the people, the state, by direction of the people can call back the Senator and appoint one who better represents the people.

From my perspective, this may have originally appeared to be a good amendment but it overall has hurt the people. The people are stuck with a bad senator now for six years. What a shame.

XVIII.

The Eighteenth Amendment provided for prohibition of the manufacture, sale, transportation, importation, and exportation of intoxicating liquors for beverage purposes. Congress and the States were given concurrent power to enforce the amendment. Elliott Ness is the only person who seemed to take the law seriously.

The amendment became effective January 16, 1920. It proved to be unsatisfactory, for many reasons. Confusion arose because of the division of police powers. Enforcement by the national government was impossible. It was urged that this amendment was in conflict with the fifth, by taking property without due process of law. What would be next, outlawing 16-oz soft drinks in NYC?

It conflicted with the provision which makes the acts of Congress the supreme law of the land. Personal liberty, it was claimed, was abridged. On this point the Supreme Court said (Corneli v. Moore, 267 Fed. 456):

"It may be a matter of regret that age-old provisions making for the liberty of action of the citizen have been encroached upon, and to a degree whittled away; but this is not a matter wherein the courts may relieve. It is a political question and not a judicial one."

In other words, the Supreme Court chose not to go along with regular Joe's. They do not always get it right!

After 13 years of trial, with increasing confusion, dissatisfaction, and expense, the Eighteenth Amendment was repealed by the Twenty-first Amendment, which became effective December 5, 1933. Prohibition was gone and Ness, God love him, hopefully retired on a great pension, which unfortunately today could not be afforded by the people.

XIX.

The Nineteenth Amendment provides that the right of United States citizens to vote shall not be denied or abridged by the United States or any state on account of sex. It was declared adopted August 26, 1920. The first proposal to amend the Constitution to provide for woman suffrage was offered by Senator Sargent, of California, in 1878, at the request of Miss Susan B. Anthony.

Fifteen States had granted complete suffrage to women before the amendment was adopted, and in all but nine of the rest they had partial suffrage. A woman was elected to the House of Representatives from Montana in 1916. Women first voted on a national scale in the presidential election of 1920, and apparently their total vote was about 6,000,000. It is believed that at least 12,000,000 women voted in 1932.

When we think of the dumbness that has been so prevalent in our government throughout time, most of the time, it was because of the perception of popular thinking, not because of animus. Blacks were freed by Abraham Lincoln along with a whole lot of white guys who never held anybody, white or black, as a slave.

These white guys were married to white or black women. When color no longer mattered from the laws on the books via amendments, bad residues in old laws were still around and still needed to be fixed. Suffrage was one of them.

Thankfully, black and woman suffrage are now part of the deal. It's been like this for over 100 years so let's get rid of the notion of racism or sexism as precepts of the US government. It has been corrected. Today at worst it is an individual thing.

Just as there are blacks and women who hate whites and men, there surely are whites and men who hate blacks and women. So, what? Should we arrest them all? This amendment is one of those necessary to remove the stigmas of sex and racism in the voting process. America has surely been trying to get itself right.

XX.

The Twentieth Amendment was adopted primarily for the purpose of abolishing "lame duck" sessions of Congress. It changes the dates when the terms of the President, senators and representatives shall begin and end. The presidential term now begins on January 20 every fourth year, and the terms of senators and representatives begin on January 3, the length of term remaining six and two years, respectively. Consequently, a new Congress convenes in the January following the presidential election of the preceding November.

Since only 17 days elapse between the convening of Congress on January 3 and the inauguration of the President on January 20, it is possible that embarrassment may arise in case of delay in counting and declaring the electoral vote, or in electing a President by the House in the event of failure of the electors to elect. The amendment provides that if the President-elect shall have died before inauguration day the Vice President-elect shall be President; and that if a President shall not have been chosen or shall have failed to qualify by inauguration day, the Vice President-elect shall act as President until a President shall have qualified. Congress is authorized to provide for filling a vacancy occurring through failure of both a President-elect and Vice President-elect to qualify, and the person selected shall act until a President or Vice President shall have qualified.

Congress has provided that it shall meet in joint session on January 6 following a presidential election, to count the electoral vote and declare the result. This allows only three days for organization of the House of Representatives by the election of a Speaker. Serious difficulties might arise if the House should fail to organize in time to count the vote, or to elect a President if that duty should fall upon it. Failure of the House to elect a President might be attended by failure of the Senate to elect a Vice President. It is quite conceivable, also, that passions might be aroused if failure to elect a President by a House controlled by one political party should be followed by election of a Vice President by a Senate controlled by another party. It is also conceivable that the two houses of Congress might deadlock upon the selection of a person to fill a vacancy in the Presidency.

XXI.

The Twenty-first Amendment repeals the Eighteenth Amendment which prohibits the transportation or importation into any state of intoxicating liquors in violation of its laws.

XXII

The 22nd amendment limits the president to only two 4-year terms in office. Before the 22nd amendment, Presidents traditionally served two terms, following the example of George Washington. Franklin D Roosevelt broke this tradition during his presidency and served four terms, as World War II and the Great Depression convinced him to run for a third and fourth term, since the country was in crisis. After FDR died in 1945, many Americans began to recognize that having a president serve more than eight years was bad for the country. This led to the 22nd amendment, which was passed by Congress in 1947 and ratified by the states by 1951

XXIII

The 23rd Amendment to the US Constitution was passed by Congress on March 29, 1961. It provides the District of Columbia with the ability to vote for president and vice-president. Up until this time, individuals who lived in the District of Columbia were unable to vote for the president since they did not live in a state and presidential elector were determined based on the number of representatives and senators a state had. This set the number of electors for the District of Columbia equal to that of the least populous state which means that it has three electors.

XXIV

The 24th amendment was important to the Civil Rights Movement as it ended mandatory poll taxes that prevented many African Americans from voting. The rationale for the amendment was that poll taxes, combined with grandfather clauses and intimidation, effectively prevented African Americans from having any sort of political power, especially in the South. When the 24th amendment passed, five southern states, Virginia, Alabama, Texas, Arkansas, and Mississippi still had poll taxes. Most Southern states, at one time or another had poll taxes and in severe cases, had cumulative poll taxes that required the voter to pay taxes not just from that year, but also previous years they had not voted.

Admittedly poll taxes are inherently unfair but Americans being lied to by government is also unfair, and unfortunately, there are American parties that try to trick the least capable of US to discern the message that they will lose their ability to live if X is not elected over Y, even if X is a rapist, a murderer, or a simple political cheat—a thief so to speak.

All men are created equal for sure, and poll taxes may not be proper but permitting the simple minded among us to vote for such important notions is also not fair as they are affected by the messages of the tricksters.

Today, we should have a means of telling a lie from the truth, and any politician who lies should be disqualified from the opportunity of office. If it is discerned by judges that such messages would cause those who would otherwise not know better that they had been lied to then, and I do not know how to do this, their votes would not count. We the People want an informed electorate to vote for important offices. We should figure out how to eliminate those who have no clue who is running from being the deciding voters.

That is the truth. Unfortunately, our laws do not force politicians to tell the truth or go to jail. Either we have huge prison penalties for lying officials in office and in their candidacies or we need poll gimmicks to prevent the easily influenced by lies to not influence important elections. You tell me how we do that? Otherwise, the least capable people in America may choose who runs our country!

XXV

If the President of the United State dies in office, the Vice President will assume the position of the presidency. Although this is the law today, this was not always the case prior to the 25th amendment. In fact, it was never actually clear in the Constitution that the Vice-President takes over for the President.

The Vice-President has taken over for the President several times in our history, usually after the president has been killed or dies of sickness and the first time this happened was when John Tyler, the 10th president, became president after William Henry Harrison died after a month as President. The 25th amendment allows for the Vice President to become president in the event of death, resignation, removal from office or impairment that prevents the current president from fulfilling his or her duties.

The Vice-presidency had been clearly defined by the 12th amendment as the running mate of the sitting president. As such, there is no risk that a member of the opposing party will gain the presidency in the event of the president being unable to serve his or her duties. Among the more important provisions of the 25th amendment are the provisions for the "Acting President."

During this condition, the Vice-President temporarily assumes the role of the President as it is assumed that the President is unable to fulfill his or her duties at the moment but will be able to in the very near future.

The 25th amendment was adopted by the states in 1967 with Nebraska and Wisconsin being the first states to ratify it and Nevada the 38th and last state needed to have a ¾ majority

XXVI

The 26th Amendment to the US Constitution was passed by Congress on March 23, 1971 and ratified on July 1, 1971, all during the Vietnam War. The amendment provided the right to vote to individuals who were eighteen years of age. Previous to this, the 14th Amendment had set the voting age at 21. Very strong feelings existed that if people were old enough to serve and die for their country, they should also be able to vote for those people sending them to war.

XXVII

The 27th Amendment to the US Constitution prohibits any law that increases or decreases the salary of members of Congress from taking effect until the start of the next set of terms of office for Representatives. It is the most recent amendment to the United States Constitution.

It was submitted by Congress to the states for ratification on September 25, 1789, and became part of the United States Constitution in May 1992, a record-setting period of 202 years, 7 months and 12 days.

As we examine rights in this book, the politicians of yesteryear submitted this item to be in the original bill of rights as the second amendment. It was rejected then and somewhat recently has passed and thus its new sequence is amendment # 27.

Conclusion

The conclusion for this chapter is mostly written by Sol Bloom. It is from his 150th Anniversary Book re-mastered by Lets Go Publish! The book is titled, *Sol Bloom's ... Epoch Story of the Constitution.*

From the time that I read his book I have been impressed with the late Congressman Bloom. He is in my opinion a 1937 version of America's founders. I have used many of his thoughts in the chapters we have already discussed. I give you many of his original thoughts in the conclusion below, though I have altered some of the notions as written to fit the times. To get the original, feel free to read Bloom's book.

https://www.amazon.com/Sol-Blooms-Epoch-Story-Constitution/dp/0989995763

Here is the Chapter Conclusion, which not so coincidentally is also the conclusion of Sol Bloom's Book on the Constitution.

"As the symmetry of arrangement and beautiful co-ordination of motion in the several governments constituting the American system may be compared with the solar system.

"As the Sun is the center of attraction and controlling power that binds and moves the planets in one system, so the People are the center and controlling power that binds and moves their governments in one system.

"The Law which the solar system obeys is not written, but its operation is partly disclosed and partly understood. The Law which the American political system obeys is partly written, for all men to read. It is the Constitution of the United States.

"The limits of the powers of the Sun and the People are not known. They have never been tested to the limit. The composition of the Sun is hidden in Nature. The composition of the People is hidden in human nature.

"Reason assumes that the Sun has powers beyond those known to us. Reason reinforced by knowledge asserts that the People have reserved powers which never have been expressed in written law.

"The United States and the States may be compared to planets revolving around their Sun, the People.

"In order to comprehend the peculiar nature of the American system it must be borne in mind that the States existed before the United States was created. It was to bind them together, to swing them into their coordinated orbits that the Union was perfected.

"Some of the powers possessed by the People are exerted in the States. Others are kept in reserve.

"The powers necessary to bind the States together in one solar Union are set forth in the Constitution. All other powers are kept in reserve.

"The States perform certain functions which the United States cannot perform. The United States performs functions which the States separately cannot perform. The People retain a sphere of personal liberties into which neither the States nor the United States can enter.

"The law which controls the solar system is divine, and therefore perfect. The law which controls the American political system is human, and therefore imperfect. But under a trial of 150 years [when Bloom wrote his book in 1937], it has been found to approach more nearly the symmetry of the law that rules the universe than any other emanation of the human mind and will.

"Several unique features of the Constitution distinguish it from any previous inventions in the art of government. Among these are: The Constitution binds individuals as well as States. Under it all individuals have equal duties and rights.

"The legislative, executive, and judicial powers are lodged in separate bodies of public servants whose powers and duties compel them to check and balance one another. No uncontrolled power is lodged in any one. The written Constitution is made paramount to any legislative, executive, or judicial authority.

"A court is created with power to hold all authorities within their allotted spheres, and this court itself is bound to remain within its allotted sphere. The Constitution contains within itself a method whereby it may be amended by the People.

"These principles, never practiced before, are the bone and sinew of a fabric suitable to a nation whose government obeys those whom it rules, and whose people rule the government which they obey."

End of Sol Bloom's Conclusion.

Don't we all wish that we could write as well as Sol Bloom. He has helped us all understand why being an American, born of the founders and of Sol Bloom's sweat labor, is such a big deal. We Americans are all so lucky!

Chapter 21 Constitutional Rights, Powers and Duties

The people or the government?

The Bill of Rights is the collective name for the first ten amendments to the United States Constitution. It helps to repeat that often when one is learning the concepts of our founding government. As you may know from earlier reading in this book, the Bill of Rights was proposed to quiet the fears of Anti-Federalists who had opposed Constitutional ratification.

The ten (originally twelve) amendments were brought forth to guarantee a number of personal freedoms (rights), limit the government's power in judicial and other proceedings, and reserve some powers to the states and the public.

Originally the amendments applied only to the federal government. However, most were subsequently applied to the government of each state by way of the Fourteenth Amendment to the Constitution, through a process known as incorporation.

Let's recap how these rights were introduced to Congress. On June 8, 1789, Representative James Madison introduced a series of thirty-nine amendments (Lots more than the twelve which were approved) to the constitution in the House of Representatives. Among his recommendations Madison proposed opening up the Constitution and inserting specific rights directly into the articles of the Constitution. His notions limited the power of Congress beginning in Article One, Section 9. At the time, the founders figured Congress had the real power and there would be no need to limit the power of the chief executive as Congress could theoretically do that by itself.

Seven of these limitations would eventually become part of the ten ratified Bill of Rights as amendments. Ultimately, on September 25, 1789, Congress approved twelve articles of amendment to the Constitution and submitted them to the states for ratification. Many of the Anti-Federalists wanted the Constitution itself, within in its main body, not in adjunct form, to delineate the rights of the people of the nation. Madison's original proposal had provided for that.

Contrary to Madison's original proposal that the articles be incorporated into the main body of the Constitution, they were eventually proposed as "supplemental" additions to it. On December 15, 1791, Articles Three–Twelve, having been ratified by the required number of states, became renumbered as Amendments One–Ten of the Constitution. These ten ratified amendments were the Bill of Rights as passed and became a part of the Constitution forever.

On May 7, 1992, after an unprecedented period of 202 years, 225 days, the original submitted and not ratified Amendment # 2, known then as Article Two crossed the Constitutional threshold for ratification and became the Twenty-Seventh Amendment and the last amendment as of 2014. As a result, the original Article One (the original 1st amendment) alone remains unratified and still pending before the states.

The Bill of Rights enumerates freedoms not explicitly indicated in the main body of the Constitution, such as freedom of religion, freedom of speech, a free press, and free assembly; the right to keep and bear arms; freedom from unreasonable search and seizure, security in personal effects, and freedom from warrants issued without probable cause; indictment by a grand jury for any capital or "infamous crime"; guarantee of a speedy, public trial with an impartial jury; and prohibition of double jeopardy.

The rights of the people

In addition, the Bill of Rights reserves for the people any rights not specifically mentioned in the Constitution and reserves all powers not specifically granted to the federal government for the people or the States. The Bill was influenced by George Mason's 1776 Virginia

Declaration of Rights, the English Bill of Rights 1689, and earlier English political documents such as Magna Charta (1215 A.D.).

The Bill of Rights had little judicial impact for the first 150 years of its existence, but was the basis for many Supreme Court decisions of the 20th and 21st centuries. One of the first fourteen copies of the Bill of Rights is on public display at the National Archives in Washington, D.C.

What specific rights / powers do we the people have and what rights / powers do we the people not have? What rights / powers does the government have and which ones does it not have? All Americans should want to know the answers to those questions.

And so, we have a ton of rights and powers to discuss in the remainder of this chapter. Since this is a book about the Bill of Rights it is a good idea to define a right as well as a power or a duty so that we get a clear picture of what the Constitution and the Bill of Rights delivers to us

What is a right? A right is a moral or legal entitlement to have or obtain something or to act in a certain way

What is a power? A power is the ability to do something or act in a particular way, especially as a faculty or quality. Also, a power can be defined as the possession of control or command over others; authority.

What is a duty? A duty is a moral or legal obligation; a responsibility. It can also be a task or action that someone is required to perform.

The following outline describes in brief the more important rights, powers, and duties recognized or established in the U.S. Constitution, in Common Law as it existed at the time the U.S. Constitution was adopted, or as implied therein.

Not included in this outline are certain "internal" or administrative rights and powers that pertain to the various elements of government within each level with respect to each other. This chapter is just big enough to give us a proper perspective on what the Constitution along with the Bill of Rights provide for all Americans.

Most of the content in this outline is supplied by the Constitution Society. We have changed some text for brevity, clarification, and / or style changes. We give our thanks to The Constitution Society for their great work: www.constitution.org

Let's continue our definitions below to set the stage for the discussion or rights, powers, and duties. Let's first examine the notion of "personhood," and then go from there.

Personhood: "Persons" are one of the two main classes which are the subject of rights, powers, and duties, the other being "citizens". Persons may be "natural" or "corporate". Yes, according to the Supreme Court of the United States (SCOTUS), corporations are to be treated as legal citizens.

"Citizens" are a subclass of "natural persons". Only persons have standing as parties under due process. Each government has the power to define what is and is not a "person" within its jurisdiction, subject to certain restrictions of Common Law and the Constitution, the 15th Amendment to which requires that it not exclude anyone based on race, color, or previous condition of servitude.

Under Common Law existing at the time of the adoption of the U.S. Constitution, "natural personhood" was considered to begin at natural birth and end with the cessation of the heartbeat. But technology has created a new situation, opening the way for statute or court decision to extend this definition and set the conditions under which personhood begins and ends.

Each government may also establish, within its jurisdiction, "corporate persons" such as governmental entities, associations, trusts, corporations, or partnerships, in addition to the Common Law "natural" persons, but the "personhood" of such corporate entities is not created by the government. Its corporate personhood derives from the personhood of its members. Corporate persons must be aggregates of natural persons.

Citizenship: Citizenship is the attribute of persons who, as members of the polity, have certain privileges and duties in addition to those they have as persons. Citizens include those born on U.S. or State territory or naturalized according to law.

Natural Rights: The classic definition of "natural rights" are "life, liberty, and property", but these need to be expanded somewhat. They are rights of "personhood", not "citizenship". These rights are not all equally basic, but form a hierarchy of derivation, with those listed later being generally derived from those listed earlier.

What is Personal Security (Life)?

(1) Not to be killed.
(2) Not to be injured or abused.

What is Personal Liberty?

(3) To move freely.
(4) To assemble peaceably.
(5) To keep and bear arms
(6) To assemble in an independent well-disciplined[13] militia.
(7) To communicate with the world.
(8) To express or publish one's opinions or those of others.
(9) To practice one's religion.
(10) To be secure in one's person, house, papers, vehicle[14], and effects against unreasonable searches and seizures.
(11) To enjoy privacy in all matters in which the rights of others are not violated.
What is Private Property?
(12) To acquire, have and use the means necessary to exercise the above natural rights and pursue happiness, specifically including:

- A private residence, from which others may be excluded.
- Tools needed for one's livelihood.
- Personal property, which others may be denied the use of.
- Arms suitable for personal and community defense.

What are non-natural rights of personhood,created by social contract?

(1) To enter into contracts, and thereby acquire contractual rights, to secure the means to exercise the above natural rights.
(2) To enjoy equally the rights, privileges and protections of personhood as established by law.
(3) To petition an official for redress of grievances and get action thereon in accordance with law, subject to the resources available thereto.
(4) To petition a legislator and get consideration thereof, subject to resources available thereto.
(5) To petition a court for redress of grievances and get a decision thereon, subject to resources available thereto.
(6) Not to have one's natural rights individually disabled except through due process of law, which includes:

(A) IN CRIMINAL PROSECUTIONS:

1. Not to be charged for a major crime but by indictment by a Grand Jury, except while serving in the military, or while serving in the Militia during time of war or public danger.
2. Not to be charged more than once for the same offense.
3. Not to be compelled to testify against oneself.

4. Not to have excessive bail required.
5. To be tried by an impartial jury from the state and district in which the events took place.
6. To have a jury of at least six for a misdemeanor, and at least twelve for a felony.
7. To a speedy trial.
8. To a public trial.
9. To have the assistance of counsel of one's choice.
10. To be informed of the nature and cause of the accusation.
11. To be confronted with the witnesses against one.
12. To have compulsory process for obtaining favorable witnesses.
13. To have each charge proved beyond a reasonable doubt.
14. To have a verdict by a unanimous vote of the jury, which shall not be held to account for its verdict.
15. To have the jury decide on both the facts of the case and the constitutionality, jurisdiction, and applicability of the law.
16. Upon conviction, to have each disablement separately and explicitly proven as justified and necessary based on the facts and verdict.
17. To have a sentence which explicitly states all disablements, and is final in that once rendered no further disablements may be imposed for the same offense.
18. Not to have a cruel or unusual punishment inflicted upon oneself.

(B) IN CIVIL CASES:

1. To trial by an impartial jury from the state and district in which the events took place where the issue in question is either a natural right or property worth more than $20.
2. In taking of one's property for public use, to be given just compensation therefor.
3. To have compulsory process for obtaining favorable witnesses.

(C) IN ALL CASES:

1. To have process only upon legal persons able to defend themselves, either natural persons or corporate persons that are represented by a natural person as agent, and who are present, competent, and duly notified, except, in cases of disappearance or abandonment, after public notice and a reasonable period of time
2. Not to be ordered to give testimony or produce evidence beyond what is necessary to the proper conduct of the process

What are Non-natural rights or citizenship, created by social contract?

(1) To enjoy equally the rights and privileges of citizenship as established by law.
(2) To vote in elections that are conducted fairly and honestly, by secret ballot.
(3) To exercise general police powers to defend the community and enforce the laws, subject to legal orders of higher-ranking officials
(4) To receive militia training.

See also List of constitutional rights.

Disabilities of minority: Certain of the above rights are restricted, or "disabled", for minors, but the definition of who is a minor and the extent to which each of these rights are disabled for minors, is limited to the jurisdiction over which each government has general legislative authority, which for the U.S. government, is "federal ground" (see below).

Minors are the only class of persons whose rights may be disabled without a need to justify the disablement as arising from the need to resolve a conflict with the rights of others, either through statute or due process.

The disablement consists of the assignment of a power to supervise the exercise of the rights under the headings of "liberty" and "property" listed above to a guardian, by default the parents, who acts as agent of the State for the purpose of nurturing the minor. The disability is normally removed by statute providing for removal when a certain age, such as 18, or condition, such as marriage, is attained.

The disabilities of minority can also be removed earlier by court order or, if statute allows, extended beyond the usual statutory expiration by court order in cases of incompetence. The right to vote is not included among the disabilities of minority, but is defined separately by law, so that removal of the disabilities of minority does not in itself affect having the right to vote.

What are Constitutional duties of persons under U.S. or State jurisdiction?

(1) To obey laws that are constitutional and applied within their proper jurisdiction and according to their intent.
(2) To comply with the terms of legal contracts to which one is a party.
(3) To tell the truth under oath.

What are Constitutional duties of citizens under U.S. or State jurisdiction?

(1) To preserve, protect, and defend the Constitution.
(2) To help enforce laws and practices that are constitutional and applied within their proper jurisdiction and according to their intent, and to resist those which are not.
(3) To serve on juries, and to render verdicts according to the constitutionality, jurisdiction, and applicability of statute and common law, and the facts of the case.

What are Constitutional duties of able-bodied citizens under U.S. or State jurisdiction?

(1) To defend the U.S. or State, individually and through service in the Militia.

(2) To keep and bear arms.To exercise general police powers to defend the community and enforce the laws, subject to legal orders of higher-ranking officials when present.

What are the Powers delegated to U.S. (National) Governmen?

A. Exclusive powers

(1) To lay and collect import duties.
(2) To pay the debts of the U.S. Government.
(3) To regulate commerce with foreign nations and Indian Tribes.
(4) To regulate commerce among the States.
(5) To regulate immigration.
(6) To establish a uniform rule of naturalization.
(7) To establish uniform laws on bankruptcy throughout the United States.
(8) To coin money and regulate its value and that of foreign coin, and to issue bills of credit.
(9) To provide for the punishment of counterfeiting the securities and current coin of the United States.
(10) To fix the standard of weights and measures.
(11) To provide and regulate postal services.
(12) To establish protection for intellectual property, including patent, copyright, and trademark rights.
(13) To constitute lower national courts.
(14) To define and punish piracies and felonies committed on the high seas, and offenses against the laws of nations.
(15) To declare war, authorize warlike activities by other than the armed forces, and make rules concerning captures.
(16) To raise, support and regulate the armed forces.
(17) To govern what part of the Militia shall be employed in the service of the United States.
(18) To exercise general legislation over federal ground, which is limited to federal territories and districts, land purchased from states with the consent of their legislatures, U.S. flag vessels on the high seas, and the grounds of U.S. embassies abroad.
(19) To guarantee a republican form of government to the States.
(20) To enter into a treaty, alliance, or confederation with a foreign state.
(21) To declare the punishment for treason.
(22) To prescribe the manner in which the acts, records, and judicial proceedings of each state shall be proved to other states and what should be done about them.
(23) To admit new states into the Union.
(24) To dispose of and make all needful Rules and Regulations respecting the Territory or other Property belonging to the United States.
(25) To make laws necessary and proper for executing the powers delegated to the U.S. government.

B. Pre-emptive but non-exclusive powers

(1) To provide for the common defense and general welfare.

(2) To provide for calling forth the Militia to execute the laws, suppress insurrections, and repel invasions.
(3) To provide for organizing, arming, and disciplining the Militia.
(4) To prescribe the times, places and manner of holding elections for members of Congress, except the places for electing senators.
(5) To conduct a census every ten years.

C. Non-pre-emptive non-exclusive powers
(1) To lay and collect excise taxes on commerce or income taxes on persons.
(2) To borrow money.

What are the Restrictions of the powers of the national Government:
(1) No exercise of powers not delegated to it by the Constitution.
(2) No payment from the Treasury except under appropriations made by law.
(3) Excises and duties must be uniform throughout the United States.
(4) Shall pass no tax or duty on articles exported from any state.
(5) No appointment of a senator or representative to any civil office which was created while he was a member of Congress or for which the amount of compensation was increased during that period.
(6) No preferences to the ports of one state over another in regulation or tax collection.
(7) No titles of nobility shall be granted by the U.S. government, or permitted to be granted to government officials by foreign states.
(8) May not protect a State against domestic violence without the request of its legislature, unless it cannot be convened, in which case, without the consent of its executive.
(9) U.S. courts do not have jurisdiction over suits against a state by citizens of another state or foreign country.

What are Powers delegated to State Governments?

A. Exclusive powers
(1) To appoint persons to fill vacancies in the U.S. Congress from that state and to hold special elections to replace them. State executive may make temporary appointments if state legislature in recess and until they reconvene, when they shall appoint a temporary replacement.
(2) To appoint the officers of its Militia.
(3) To conduct the training of its Militia.

B. Non-exclusive powers
(1) To prescribe the times, places and manner of holding elections for members of Congress.

What are restrictions of the powers of the State Governments?
(1) State constitutions and laws may not conflict with any provision of the U.S. Constitution or U.S. laws pursuant to it.

(2) May not exercise powers not delegated to the State government by the State Constitution.
(3) May not make anything but gold or silver coin a tender in payment of debts.
(4) May not pass a law impairing the obligation of contracts.
(5) May not grant a title of nobility.
(6) May not collect imposts or duties on imports or exports without consent of Congress, except fees necessary to cover the costs of inspections and paid to the U.S. Treasury.
(7) May not lay a duty on tonnage.
(8) May not keep troops or ships of war in time of peace or make war without the consent of Congress, unless actually invaded and in imminent danger that does not admit of delay.
(9) May not make a compact or agreement with another state of the U.S. or with a foreign state without the consent of Congress.

What are duties of the State Governments?
(1) Must provide a republican form of government to their citizens.
(2) Must conduct honest and fair elections, by secret ballot.
(3) Must give full faith and credit to the public acts, records, and judicial proceedings of every other state, and recognize the privileges and immunities granted thereby.
(4) Must extradite a person charged with a crime in another state to that state.
(5) Must organize and train their militias.

What are restrictions of the powers of all Governments:
(1) Shall not disable any natural or constitutional right without due process of law, and then only to the extent necessary to avoid infringing the rights of others.
(2) Shall not deny any person within its jurisdiction equal protection of the laws.
(3) Shall not suspend habeas corpus, except in case of rebellion of invasion and the public safety may require it.
(4) Shall not issue a search warrant but on probably cause, supported by an oath or affirmation, and particularly describing the place to be searched, and the person or things to be seized.
(5) Shall not arrest members of Congress, except for treason, felony, or breach of the peace, while their house is in session.
(6) Shall not question a member of Congress on anything he says during a speech or debate in his house.
(7) Shall not pass any bill of attainder or ex post facto law.
(8) Shall allow no slavery or involuntary servitude except as punishment for a crime of which the party shall have been duly convicted.
(9) Shall not deny or abridge the right to vote to any person on account of race, color, previous condition of servitude, sex, for failure to pay any tax, or on account of age if older than 18.

(10) Shall not exercise any power in an unreasonable manner or for other than a legitimate public purpose, as partially indicated in the Preamble. (No power is "plenary", and discretion can be abused.)

What are some arguably needed national powers?
(1) To regulate the manufacture, distribution, operation, and disposition of aircraft and spacecraft, the regulation of their crews, and the definition and punishment of crimes committed on U.S. registered aircraft or spacecraft or on aircraft or spacecraft operating in U.S. airspace.
(2) To regulate cabled or wireless communications beyond a distance of 1 kilometer.
(3) To regulate the production, distribution, and use of nuclear energy, and electric energy transmitted more than 1 kilometer.
(4) To limit tort liability on commerce and commercial articles subject to U.S. regulation of their manufacture.
(5) To pre-emptively pass and enforce laws needed to conserve wildlife and natural resources, to protect the climate and natural environment, to prevent an excess of population, and to regulate public health and workplace safety.
(6) To provide for the punishment of abuses of power by any official, agent, or employee of, or contractor for, any institution of government, and specifically any violations of the Constitution and laws pursuant thereto.
(7) To provide for the punishment of abuses of the natural rights of persons by other persons, in the event that those abuses, if the occurred on state ground, are not prosecuted by a State government.
(8) To define "due process" to include the elements given above which are not now explicit in the U.S. Constitution.
(9) To define the arms to which persons have a right to keep and bear as including "all those weapons which may be carried by one person and which might be useful or necessary to defend oneself or the community, except weapons of mass destruction such as bombs, heavy missiles or artillery, or biological, chemical, or nuclear agents which may cause lasting injury or death."
(10) To make explicit that only natural persons or corporate persons composed of natural persons may be the subject of due process in any civil or criminal proceeding.

NOTES: Feel free to go to www.constitution.org/powright.htm to see their whole section on rights. In this, they show a series of notes associated with the delineated rights, powers, and duties shown above.

FURTHER COMMENT
by the Constitution Society—very interesting:

Note that there is no right to marry or bear children included among any of the rights listed above. It is not a "natural" right, because natural rights are only rights of individuals, and exercise of a "right" to marry, without the consent of the other, would be an assault.

Since consent is required, it is a matter of contract, and contractual rights are created by the community, even if it is a "community" of only two persons. Since the community is normally a larger polity, and since all legal contracts are agreements not only between the contracting parties, but also with the entire community, therefore the community has the power to regulate marriage and childbirth, and has exercised that power since time immemorial, for the benefit of the community.

Note also that the fundamental unit of the social contract is the local community, ward, or village. These may aggregate into a larger "state" or "federal union", but the basis is agreement among those who are in direct contact with one another.

It is sometimes thought that "the Constitution" consists only of the written document. This is not so. The title "The Constitution of the United States" was added after the document was adopted, but "constitution" meant the "basic legal order", and the Constitution consists of both the written document and the common law at the time the document was adopted, which is here referred to as the Common Law in caps. Now, the written document does supersede the Common Law where they might be in conflict, but it does not replace it, and courts must refer to the Common Law for guidance where the written document is silent or ambiguous.

In addition to the written document and the Common Law, the Constitution also includes Treaties, which, although they are valid only insofar as they are not in conflict with the written Constitution, are superior to both the Common Law and to State constitutions and laws, to the extent that those might be in conflict with the Treaties. Thus, some of the Treaties that have been adopted extend and clarify some of the rights, powers, and duties provided in the written Constitution. For example, that is how "federal ground" is extended to include coastal waters out to a certain distance from shore, and the grounds of U.S. embassies abroad, and how the rights of the people are amplified by the Charter of the United Nations and by various bilateral and multilateral Treaties that extend civil and commercial rights to U.S. citizens abroad.

On its website, www.constitution.org/powright.htm, the Constitution society provides a number of diagrams to help clarify the relationship among the various elements of law in the U.S. legal system.

Each element is superior to the one below it, although state constitutions are derived from their people, not from the U.S. Constitution. Although not shown, each element also includes the body of writings and recorded speeches of the legislators, diplomats, and judges who wrote the constitutions, treaties, laws, and court decisions, which clarify their intent, and which must be accepted as the basis of interpreting the words as originally meant and understood when there is confusion or dispute over their meaning.

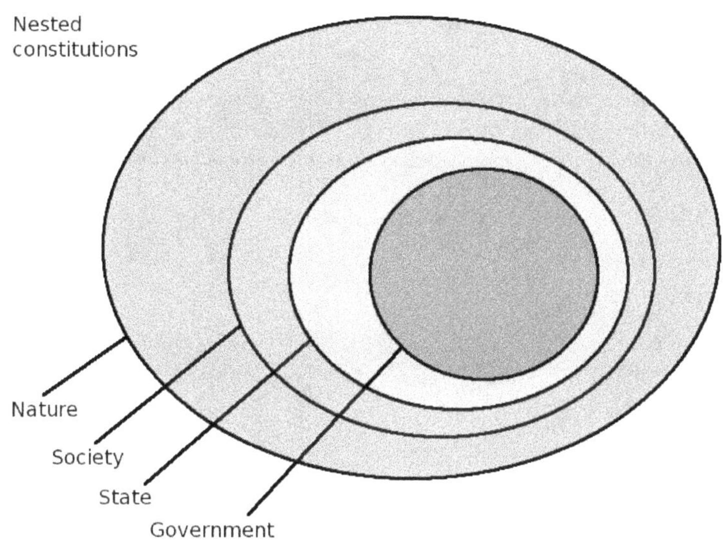

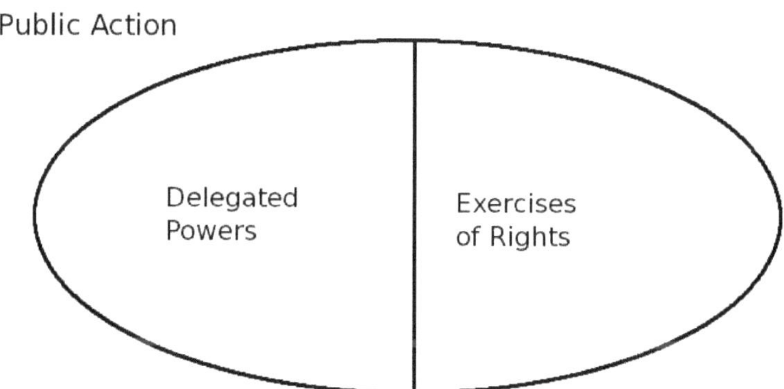

Each delegation of a power restricts rights.
Each declaration of a right restricts delegated powers.

A right (immunity) may be expressed as a restriction
on a power, and a power as a restriction on a right.

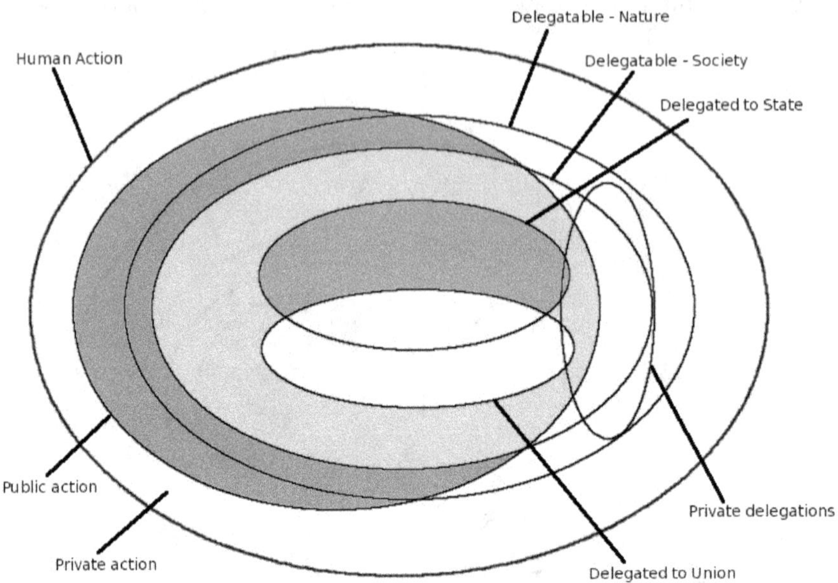
Delegatable - Nature
Human Action
Delegatable - Society
Delegated to State
Public action
Private delegations
Private action
Delegated to Union

Chapter 22 Bill of Rights Makes the Constitution OK for All!

The fight over the Bill of Rights

Now, that you and I have exhaustingly traversed multiple chapters, in search of the perfect founding of our nation along with a "perfect" Bill of Rights, should we believe that we have found it? I say yes!

The Constitution of the United States of America contains the Bill of Rights. Not only does it contain the whole Bill of Rights but it is based on a long line of other historical documents that add even more meaning to the Constitution and American rights as we find ourselves at times trying to understand exactly what the founders meant here and there. And, thus it has been quite proper to discuss most of these documents before we move to the real purpose of this book, The US Bill of Rights.

The "perfect Bill of Rights," is thus based on the "perfect Constitution." In its own rules, the Constitution prescribes a way for it to be changed, as long as the people agree. Who can ask for anything more?

In order for the Constitution to have been ratified and to become the operating supreme law of the Land of the USA, the founders convinced detractors that they would use the rules in the Constitution itself to change it to suit the detractor's needs. The Bill of Rights in fact, was the first set of changes to the US Constitution, and it satisfied the objections of the original detractors. If the founders had not done some good convincing, the Constitution would exist only in the history books and not as the law of the land.

The Constitution offers no opportunity for the congress or the president to choose to act other than directed by the articles within this document as well as the laws enacted by the Congress. In terms of the forty-fourth President, we know that there are a number of accusations of lawlessness. Nobody other than the people can change the Constitution—even the president of the United States, as hard as he may try.

The laws broken by the prior administration include violations of the pure Constitution and a number of other laws that have been enacted by Congress, which the past president, as all presidents has taken an oath to enforce. The past president had no problem with calling a weak Congress's bluff and so he chose his laws carefully, and thus, he reigned, un-impeached.

However, more and more citizens have found that the lawlessness of the Executive Branch was a little too much to stomach. In the America that the people have understood for years, they did not have a need to demanding Congress act to assure that the Constitution in totality is upheld and not disregarded as trivial by the president. The election of Donald J. Trump over Hillary R. Clinton for some in Congress was the first time that they got to fully understand the frustrations of the American people with a lawless administration.

The Constitution, though a phenomenally "more perfect" instrument of government for America than the Articles of Confederation, is still not 100% perfect. Nothing is perfect! As I like to say in its defense, it is more perfect than any other supreme body of law in any other country, including Bimini, which is a beautiful island in the Bahamas—where I think I would rather be than right here, right now!

If this were not so, I too would definitely be seeking refuge in Bimini, or the next most free country in the world. Right now, because of our Constitution, and the expressed Bill of Rights, we would find the only country that provides full freedom and liberty in all cases to be the United States of America. Though some politicians may have bought the stamp, there is no expiration date on the United States.

Americans paying attention know that the best set of laws for both the hoi polloi (regular people) and the hoity-toity (the elite among us) is our one of a kind US Constitution including its Bill of Rights and subsequent amendments.

The Bill of Rights is essential in that it spells out in bold detail, the fundamental rights of all Americans including the rights of free assembly, free speech, freedom to practice religion, and many other rights including the right to bear arms. Some presidents of recent time would like to do away with these rights.

Many ask why, with such a fine Constitution is a separate *"Bill of Rights"* required? If the Constitution is almost perfect, why was it not enough? Why is it not enough? "Why did we ever need a *Bill of Rights*? We have broached this subject in past chapters but let's take it head on again.

In this modern era, where all traditional values are questioned, there is a film and a video game known as the *Bill of Rights.* Perhaps you know of this. Perhaps you have seen it or heard about it. Both media notions (film & video game) attempt to tell the story about a struggle among the founders and the framers of the US Constitution that nearly tore the nation apart. We have discussed this but let's go again.

It was even before the US had a Constitution to assure its future. Toward the end of the 16-minute documentary, the *Bill of Rights* is described as "absolutely essential to our national character."

When the founders were founding the nation, there was no notion of political parties, and that is why the brave men of those times were able to come together to delineate a set of laws that would be able to guide America forever. There were no Republicans and there were no Democrats. There was no partisan politics because there were no partisans. The founders built it that way. Everybody was for America.

Even then, of course there was the risk of a scoundrel in an important office, who might be un-American, and that scoundrel, even if he were the president, himself, might choose to ignore the laws of the country, passed or not passed in his or her administration.

Therefore, the folks at that time, some who believed the Constitution was perfect, and others who thought that our rights needed to be declared outwardly in a positive sense, needed to come together.

The Constitution gave the people all the power but to be fair, specific important rights which many call freedoms and liberties, were not delineated. And, so an errant judge in the future, wrong as he or she might be, could decree that there is no right in the Constitution guaranteeing your freedom of speech or assembly. The judge would be wrong but, then what happens when you find yourself in prison? What do you have to say you have the right?

The Bill of Rights therefore specifically, forcefully, and more authoritatively defines the fundamental rights of the American people. Some people in 1787 had a major issue about whether the US Constitution restricted government powers sufficiently enough to assure that Americans had perpetual liberty under the law. Today's citizens can understand why!

If Government had no power to restrict the power of the people, then why should the people need a specific bill of rights? The simple answer is that after hundreds of years of tyranny in their home countries, the colonists trusted nobody, and they therefore recognized the possibility of an errant judge or powerful government of the future misunderstanding the Constitution, and going it alone without the Congress or the people.

The framers of The Constitution gave no implicit rights to government other than those so enumerated specifically in the Constitution. There were few of these as enumerated in prior chapters. So, many of the framers did not believe that the people needed a bill of rights since government could theoretically never take away the inalienable rights the people already possessed.

The Constitution gave the government no power to override the will of the people. Others were concerned that since people are people, scoundrels might emerge as leaders and the people would have no backup column to present to prove their rights. And, so many smart Americans looked for a specific Bill of Rights! I think we are better off with it than we would be without it.

Implication or Specification?

The battle of whether a Bill of Rights was necessary during the founding and framing of the Constitution is a matter of implication or specification. Those who believed the government was sufficiently verboten from taking away individual liberty saw no reason to specify (specification) the liberties that could not be taken away.

Their answer was "no liberties" can be taken from the people since the Constitution in raw form, un-amended, implicitly defers rights not given to the government as rights which the people implicitly possess. Yet, implicit or explicit, when quoted, we all like to have an explicit quote upon which to base our contention.

Well, the explicits and the implicits got their day of discussion, and our founders worked it out for the good of all to come up with something that would work. Out of their compromise (The Great Compromise) came one of our nation's most central documents and the foundation for some of our most celebrated freedoms. The document produced to represent their thoughts is forever known as the ***Bill of Rights.***

Whether it was needed logically or not needed logically, it is the Bill of Rights nonetheless. It guaranteed the ratification of The Constitution. It was enough to convince the patriots that the Constitution was perfect enough to be approved.

They felt the base Constitution was not enough

Americans wanted written assurances that the rights they fought for as colonists against Britain in the American Revolution would never be taken away. They believed their rights should be protected by a written document. The Bill of Rights plus the Constitution serve that purpose. Add the additional 17 amendments and you've got a winning trifecta.

Without and explicit bill that listed the rights of the people, some of the states had refused to ratify the Constitution. They did not like that in its first cut, a national Bill of Rights was not included. Thus, the Bill of Rights was deemed to be an essential ingredient to having a Constitution pass the states for ratification.

Without the *Bill of Rights,* we would have never been able to ratify the Constitution and thus we would never have been able to add the necessary stability to our nation to fend of all foes and grow more and more powerful. The Constitution and the specifics in the *Bill of Rights* and the other seventeen amendments have helped our country survive during the times of instability, confusion, and partial insanity concerning how to properly organize and run the nation.

The *Bill of Rights* was carved out after the Constitution had been written. And, though it is deemed by many to be an integral "part" of the Constitution, when offered to the people, it was created independently of the Constitution and presented as an add-on, though a very necessary add-on.

The *Bill of Rights* indeed consists of the first ten approved / ratified amendments to the US Constitution. The original framers trusted that we would never turn on the precepts in the Constitution. Those insisting on the need for a Bill of Rights wanted to assure themselves that we could not even find a minor loophole in the Constitution to limit our rights.

We all know, and quite often in this book, we have demonstrated how the Constitution guarantees every American certain basic rights including: freedom of speech, freedom of religion, the right to assembly, the right to a jury trial, etc. These and many other rights are implicitly protected by our Constitution. But these freedoms, though implicit, were not explicitly stated in the original version of the Constitution. It took the *Bill of Rights* to mention them explicitly.

You may have already read the full Constitution. If so, you know that nothing was written in the Constitution to implicitly or specifically grant the freedoms in the Bill of Rights to all Americans. In fact, as noted, many of the Framers of the Constitution were dead set against including such a bill in the document even if provided as amendments. Like the old TV ad once said, the framers would answer: "It's in there!"

The framers were very smart people. They knew that when they had written the Constitution, they had implicitly granted all those provisions in the Bill of Rights simply by denying government such rights. In truth, implicit provisions are far more powerful and long-serving than those explicitly provided. But, with anything implicit, the government must be even more honest. With "explicit," government would have no choice.

Honest regular people at that time, and even in this time, looking for truth have a tough time understanding and trusting implicit notions. And, so the explicit provisions of the Bill of Rights helped many Americans, who did not profess to be Constitutional scholars to lean towards the ratification of the Constitution when ten important rights of the people were explicitly noted.

Thus, as the debate ensued, the non-trusting was compelled by their very nature to demand as many explicit provisions from the new government as possible. The colonists did not trust any government at the time—even if their favorite neighbor were president.

As we all know, humans have limited attention spans. Worse than that, historical governments have most often gone bad over time. So, why would the regular folks in America back those wanting votes for the Constitution without "proper" guarantees for liberty and freedom over time?

And, so a look back does say that a Bill of Rights needed to be created and added to the Constitution. James Madison, one of the major authors of the Federalist Papers, and a great patriot, who eventually became the fourth President of the United States, was enlisted to write many of the precepts in the Bill of Rights. Like Alexander Hamilton, he was a phenomenal writer. He is credited with being the primary author of the Constitution and so he is known by historians as the "Father of the Constitution."

Ironically, Madison, in his personal thoughts, did not think a Bill of Rights was necessary. He took issue, though lightly, with those who felt that the Constitution needed to grant rights. Instead, he felt that the people had all the rights, according to the Constitution and the government had no rights other than those explicitly granted by the people. Yet, Madison was also a reasonable man.

Madison would have been against any Bill of Rights and the document that emerged from the Constitutional Convention in 1787 (The Constitution) reflected his full conviction. He believed the Constitution as it was written already spelled out what the Federal Government could do and could not do. He believed that if it wasn't in that document, it wasn't any of the Federal Government's business. No further protection was necessary. He was right logically, but as noted *implicit* was not a convincing argument for the people. I thank the Lord that Madison changed his mind.

Madison would have been fervently in favor of a Bill of Rights if he lived in the 19th, 20th, or 21st century. James Madison never met a 20th or 21st Century leftist politician looking for an excuse to break through the limitations on government provided in the Constitution to further the cause of communism.

These scoundrels love their rights yet want the rights of others taken away to suit their selfish interests. Some, even today, believe that the Bill of Rights has only postponed the villains, who sometimes even outwardly shows disdain for the freedoms granted to Americans by the Constitution.

As recently as late May 2014, for example, the past president, who claims even today to be a constitutional scholar, challenged the notion of Article II of the Constitution regarding two Senators from each state. The President said it is unfair that hugely populated Democratic States such as New York and California get just two Senators when they have lots more people. If you are reading this book in 2017, it would save some research for you to know that the past president, who no longer presides as I am writing this book, is a leftist long before he is a happy American.

There was concern by me and others that this President, with a lack of any deep love for America and the Constitution, try by Executive Order to change the Constitution? We are very pleased that he ran out of time.

The President had already done this with other laws such as those pertaining to immigration and social issues. This, of course is why his administration was considered lawless. It helps to remember that many colonists were concerned that a strong national government was a threat to individual rights and that a president might attempt to become a king, and that strengthened their demand for more explicit rights. Pre-Obama this was not ever an issue in America.

Thankfully no American President so far at least, has ever tried to convince the people he or she should be King or Queen of America. The people were concerned that if this past president's surrogate became president then we might one day soon have a queen. Her name would not be Diana or Camilla but it might be Hillary. Somebody came by and trumped her efforts to be Queen of America!

Because of things we have seen and inactions we have suffered from a wimpy do-nothing Congress, the implicit v explicit dialogue results are in. To most conservative Americans, it is far better to explicitly state rights than to have a politician motivated by political opportunism take matters into their own hands.

Why is it that the courts, using impartiality and "superior" judgment today always break decisions on party lines? Why is it that America and Americans are not the primary focus of the legislature and the courts?

Well, this is not the right book to fully discuss this particular matter, but if I had my way, I would fire the press first. They are so corrupt that they stink like dead fish. Congress is only a short whiff away from being as bad. Would it not be wonderful if political party affiliation and agendas were not how the courts or the Senate or the House would decide issues that are substantive to citizens?

The leaders and the people in colonial time had integrity as a real virtue. Their moms and dads helped them gain such virtue. Even those not on your side were good people and good enough to work for compromises that helped all Americans—not just the Democratic Party.

George Mason, a Virginia delegate vigorously disagreed with James Madison on the notion of a Bill of Rights, yet both were honorable in their disagreement. Mason was not so sure that the new government would provide anything better than the rights the British had provided, and then took back when it was convenient. Madison knew the inherent logic in the Constitution should work for all Americans.

Despite being wounded in spirit and in their wallets, Americans in the eighteenth century all knew that a long and bloody war to win independence had only recently ended. Though Madison et al believed that they had protected Americans with the magical text of The Constitution, Mason and others wanted to explicitly ensure that the new government could not erase the freedoms the patriots had fought so hard to secure.

George Mason declared that he would rather "chop off my right hand" than support a Constitution that did not include a Bill of Rights. What a great patriot!

If we are looking for forefathers of things like Articles and Declarations and Constitutions, we might well credit George Mason as the *Father of the Bill of Rights,* regardless of how active his pen was in the process.

Depending on your level of trust in the positive precepts of the Constitution as originally written, it is reasonable to believe that the more assurances of freedom the better. Those patriots looking for more assurances won and the major product of their work, The Bill of Rights was added to the Constitution as the first ten amendments on December 15, 1791.

The fact that the Constitution did not include a Bill of Rights to specifically protect Americans' hard-won rights had certainly sparked the most heated debates during the ratification process. Now that we know there is such a Bill; what rights do they give?

Let's go over a few for a second or third time as all of us have a tendency to forget important things until we realize how important they really are.

Rights from the Bill of Rights

As previously noted, the Bill of Rights are the first ten amendments (changes) to the United States Constitution. Madison saw no real problem with the Bill of Rights other than redundancy; for he already believed they existed implicitly within the Constitution.

Rather than risk destroying the Constitution, Jefferson, out of town during the debate about the Bill of Rights, wrote to Madison advocating their inclusion: "Half a loaf is better than no bread. If we cannot secure all our rights, let us secure what we can." So, Madison introduced the Bill of Rights as a series of amendments on June 8, 1789 in the First Federal Congress.

Who wrote the Bill of Rights? George Mason, who would not sign the Constitution without the Bill of Rights and James Madison, who felt they were not needed, are considered by historians to be among the two primary authors of the twelve articles in the original Bill of Rights.

Ten of the amendments of the twelve were ratified without much debate and they became the Bill of Rights in 1791. These amendments specify rights of citizens explicitly by their content and implicitly by "further" limiting the powers of the federal government. They protect the rights of all citizens, residents and visitors on United States territory. More people today understand the Bill of Rights even more than those that understand the full impact of the US Constitution.

About the Bill of Rights?

So, what is meant by the term Bill of Rights? It represents the full notion of the first ten amendments to the United States Constitution. Amendments are supposed to be changes even though Madison believed these ten Amendments, and the rights they gave American citizens existed implicitly in the original drafting of the US Constitution. Madison saw the Bill as being redundant; but redundancy on a topic such as liberty and freedom was OK with him. In the end, James Madison was OK with the Bill of Rights.

These amendments, known as the Bill of Rights were specific rights to be granted to citizens even if they had not conceived that they already had the rights simply because the Constitution granted no such rights to government.

The Bill of Rights in summary, even today, explicitly limits the federal government's powers. It protects the rights of the people by preventing Congress from abridging freedom of speech, freedom of the press, freedom of assembly, freedom of religious worship, and the right to bear arms, and many other rights as noted in the ten very specific amendments.

For example, the Bill of Rights prevents unreasonable search and seizure, cruel and unusual punishment, and self-incrimination, and it guarantees due process of law and a speedy public trial with an impartial jury. Implicitly the Constitution itself gave the people these rights but for the people, having the issue presented and the right demonstrated meant a lot more than wondering what was what.

In addition, the Bill of Rights states that "the enumeration in the Constitution, of certain rights, shall not be construed to deny or disparage others (rights) retained by the people," and reserves all powers not specifically granted to the Federal government to the citizenry or States.

The original Ten Amendments to the Constitution, The Bill of Rights was introduced by Madison and passed by Congress September 25, 1789. These amendments came into effect when three/fourths of the states ratified them on December 15, 1791—four years after the Constitution had been created.

Chapter 23 The Federalist Papers

The Constitution—great but not perfect!

Most Americans already know that our nation today is in peril; yet many Americans choose not to believe this is the case. For those who see it as it is, tyranny in our highest federal offices, the existence of the deep state, it would help for all of US to do as you are doing with this book. Reread the Declaration of Independence and the Constitution, and the Bill of Rights. We have examined each of these historical documents in detail in this book. And so, all readers—at this point of this book—especially those who have read the underlying documents—are already qualified to see the current goings-on, as pure tyranny.

Would the founders have expected this? To know more about what was on the minds of the founders when they put forth this great Constitution, and the Bill of Rights, there is a real way in which we can almost crawl into the pure minds of our founders.

As you have learned so far, the founders and the Constitution Framers never expected corruption to interfere with the many checks and balances they had prepared for America and had written into the Constitution and the Bill of Rights. Yet, here we are, we just exited an administration in which we had a lawless and lying presidential administration and tyranny that we had not seen since England was our master. To make matters worse, we had and still have a Congress full of wimps, who will not assure the Law of the Land.

To know what the founders thought in the 1780's when all of the great ideas were flowing, it would help us all to read or reread The Federalist Papers, a series of 85 essays written by Alexander Hamilton, John Jay, and James Madison. They explain the thought process on all aspects of the Constitution. Let's Go Publish (LGP), my publisher, has a new edition of the Federalist Papers that uses the same words but with shorter paragraphs, making the papers far easier to read. It is available at www.amazon.com/author/brianwkelly. The Federalist papers in original form are also available for reading in many places on the Internet for free. By reading the Federalist Papers you will better understand the Constitution.

You can read the entire set of The Federalist Papers online. The following URL is excellent:
http://www.constitution.org/fed/federa00.htm

One morning when I was researching this book, Glenn Beck on his show suggested that the Constitution is a gift from God. It is indeed. The Federalist Papers are a means of understanding this document more than otherwise possible.

The Constitution in base form is 4,543 words; with the 27 amendments, it is 7,891 words. The Federalist papers were written to explain why the Constitution should be ratified and so it was written for the 4,543-word basic Constitution. The first complete book with all 85 essays on the papers from 1787 contains 189,954 pages. The irony is that it took Hamilton, Jay, and Madison more than 40 times the number of words to explain the Constitution than the number of words in the Constitution itself.

Back in 1787, a number of states had sent detailed written plans for the Constitution along with their delegates to the Constitutional Convention in Philadelphia. The Convention began on May 25, 1787 and lasted until September 17, 1787.

On September 17, 1787, the state delegates approved the Constitution as written by Madison et al in its final form. The Framers had completed their work and sent the document back to the individual states to be ratified. They then adjourned the convention. Without ratification, however, the Constitution was not yet the law of the land.

For Mrs Church from her Sister Elizabeth Hamilton

THE

FEDERALIST:

A COLLECTION

OF

ESSAYS,

WRITTEN IN FAVOUR OF THE

NEW CONSTITUTION,

AS AGREED UPON BY THE FEDERAL CONVENTION, SEPTEMBER 17, 1787.

IN TWO VOLUMES.

VOL. I.

NEW-YORK:

PRINTED AND SOLD BY J. AND A. M'LEAN,
No. 41, HANOVER-SQUARE,
M,DCC,LXXXVIII.

Convincing the Public

The commencing of the Federalist Papers began shortly thereafter. The writing of the papers was commissioned by Alexander Hamilton, a great patriot, who knew he could not write all of the arguments necessary for the people to choose to agree to back the Constitution. Hamilton, and John Jay, and James Madison, together wrote The Federalist Papers to defend and explain the newly drafted Federal Constitution, and to promote its ratification in the state of New York. A group of folks just as patriotic but who were dead-set against the Constitution became known as the Anti-Federalists.

Each of the papers was written as an essay, but when published they became articles in New York newspapers and magazines. Because New York at the time and to this day is a huge and prosperous state, their being published in NY was very important for the ratification of the Constitution. Thus, for the writers, it was the major objective of their attention at the time. Though the papers were written for New York, they were read in all the states prior to ratification of the Constitution.

The Federalist Papers, written by Alexander Hamilton, John Jay, and James Madison answered the debated questions as posed by the opposition in great detail while copious detractors wrote their own essays / articles in rebuttal. They were completed in 1788 and published in book form together.

As noted above, and worth repeating, the opposition articles collectively are known as the Anti-Federalist Papers. Many were published in the press so as to offer other thoughts on such an important issue.

Nowhere was the furor over the proposed Constitution in the few states of the US more intense than in New York. Governor George Clinton was very concerned that the state's influence would be compromised at the Constitutional Convention.

The NY Legislature selected State Supreme Court Judge Robert Yates and John Lansing, Speaker of the NY Assembly; to attend the convention. Both were well known Anti-Federalists. Their selection was seen by many as a way for New York to be able to outvote Alexander Hamilton.

There were those, such as Yates and Lansing, whose opposition to the new document was based on their view that the Constitution diminished the rights that Americans had won in the Revolution. The Federalist Papers presented a view that this was not true while the Anti-Federalist Papers, also displayed in popular newspapers of the day, presented a view that the Constitution was bad for America and offered its specific rationale.

Alexander Hamilton became fearful that the cause for the Constitution might be lost in his home state of New York. And to be repetitive for learning purposes, this was his purpose in putting together the Federalist Papers.

Hamilton published his first "Federalist" essay in the New York Independent Journal on October 27, 1787

The Federalist, also called The Federalist Papers, has served two very different purposes in American history. The 85 essays succeeded in helping to persuade doubtful New Yorkers (as well as the public in the other states), despite the well written efforts of the Anti-Federalists, to ratify the Constitution.

Today, The Federalist Papers help the rest of US to more clearly understand what the writers of the Constitution had in mind when they drafted this amazing document more than 225 years ago.

"America- if we cannot define Liberty, we cannot defend it. If we cannot define tyranny, we cannot defeat it-" KrisAnne Hall http://krisannehall.com/man-africa/

"If a nation expects to be ignorant and free, in a state of civilization, it expects what never was and never will be."
- Thomas Jefferson

Let us all be smart. Let us pay attention, and let us continue to be free with unlimited liberty in the finest country that God ever permitted to be founded.

Chapter 24 You're Not Alone Fighting Political Corruption

The four personal to-dos to halt corruption

We used the space of this book to point out the massive corruption in our government. We did not stop there. Most Americans already know our one-time reasonably pure government is corrupt to the hilt. So, we discussed a four-part program for Americans to exercise in order to gain back a true representative democracy.

1. Do not trust the government – especially at the top
2. Pay attention to what government officials are doing
3. Learn your rights (Constitution & Bill of Rights)
4. Take positive action to end corruption

The major tact that we suggested for item # 4 was to throw out the bad guys. Don't look for an excuse to keep them because they are corrupt, or we would not be in the mess we are today in the US. We must throw them all out if we must. That is our right but we must take this right very seriously to protect all of our other rights.

You will be pleased to know, I am sure that I am not the only person in the US and elsewhere across the globe that is trying to find a solution to this most insidious problem. The four-point plan I outline above is a great start. The founders never expected Americans to sit idly by while scoundrels in government destroyed the country. But there is more for sure that we can do and this chapter focuses on some efforts by others to reign in the frauds and the cheats and all the dirty politicians that are mucking up our great country.

Our focus is of course the United States. But this is not to say that other countries do not have similar issues. Our objective is not anarchy and the solutions that we put forth assume that the intent is to get rid of the corruption and not the government.

Besides the four personal points there are a number of things that require a concerted effort along with some honest power brokers since the issues are far too pervasive for a few individuals to tackle and win. But, everything begins with individuals and that is why I outlined the four points above.

Eliminating corruption at most levels of U.S. government requires a complete overhaul of the way elections are financed and implemented. If we continually had good and honest candidates and a system that did not reward dishonesty, we would not be in this mess and so we must seek to amend our processes to help get us get back to where we need to be.

We cannot permit the secrecy that goes on in the system and instead we need strict transparency regulations. Corruption requires secrecy and the ability to use money or power to influence elected representatives to vote against the best interests of their constituents is well served when "nobody knows."

So far, this book has helped us understand how the system currently works. In our republic, as a constitutional representative democracy, we the voters elect representatives. However, corporations, special interests, lobbyists, and wealthy individuals spends lots of money to finance election campaigns.

We hope we get good candidates to represent our interests. They hope that they get malleable candidates who talk a good game but who will serve them alone and not the people. In other words, they expect the representative to represent their own best interests rather than the best interests of voters. They use the lobby system to let representatives know how they should vote if they want continued campaign support or other favors.

What I've described in just a few words is a corrupt system in which the corruption has been tacitly legalized. The fix is simple if we can get the corrupt officials to change the methods of election. We need to simply make voters pay for campaigns by way of tax dollars. Then, we need to fully regulate lobbyists so that any interaction with an elected representative must be publicly documented. The first amendment guarantees lobbyists (and everyone else) the right to free speech, which by definition is public speech. However, there is no provisions in any law to permit bribing of public officials. We need to call it like it is and bribery must be a major crime with real punishment and real shame.

There are lots of specific recommendations that some fine authors have been written about in books and great articles on the Internet. If we the people can mount a write-in campaign to have our public officials implement what is necessary to make our system clean, we have a great opportunity. There are those among us with major resources. They can help finance a campaign against corruption that is national and massive in scope. It is up to us to make sure they know that we are serious.

Here are two great sites. The first describes the problem and the second offers a fine solution. We provide most of the text from these sites in the rest of this chapter.

https://act.represent.us/sign/the-solution/
https://act.represent.us/sign/the-problem

The above web site provides us with more good news. There is already an active group dedicated to end political corruption. It has a name that is hard to forget and a web site (above) to match called

represent.us.

What do they do?

They bring together conservatives, progressives, and everyone in between to pass powerful anti-corruption laws that stop political bribery, end secret money, and fix our broken elections. You can learn more about the policies we support at anticorruptionact.org

How do they do it?

We had a saying at the IBM Office in Scranton PA when it was still part of the IBM Company. We were feeling a lot like stepchildren in the big IBM Company. One of our salesmen when confronted by an IBM executive about not promising immediate action on a customer situation so the on-site executive would look like a hero at the customer meeting, told this particular IBMer after the meeting in no uncertain terms. "Nothing happens overnight in Scranton." I have never forgotten that." e

Nothing happens overnight anywhere. It takes a plan and it takes persistence and time to accomplish anything worthwhile in life.

Together, Represent.US is going around the Congress. Congress (A major part of The Swamp) won't do anything to hurt themselves. Represent. Us members bring powerful anti-corruption reforms to the ballot, where the people can vote for them directly. (No politicians required.)

In 2014, for example, conservatives and progressives worked together to pass America's first citywide Anti-Corruption Act in Tallahassee, Florida. Since then, voters have passed Anti-Corruption Acts and Resolutions in 30 cities and states across America.

In 2016, Represent.Us members passed the first statewide Anti-Corruption Act in South Dakota. Soon after, the state legislature brazenly repealed it.

In 2017/2018, the members are fighting back in South Dakota with a statewide Anti-Corruption Amendment that politicians can't repeal or change. And together, they're headed to the ballot in 4-8 more states and dozens of cities nationwide. Support this group and groups like it. Nothing in life worthwhile is easy.

One of the bulwarks of this program is called The American Anti-Corruption Act (AACA) Don't you just like the sound of that?

The **American Anti-Corruption Act** (AACA) is sometimes shortened to the **Anti-Corruption Act.** It is a piece of model legislation constructed to limit the influence of money in American politics by overhauling lobbying, transparency, and campaign finance laws. It is not at all frivolous and it has great potential to help solve the plague of corruption in American government.

It was crafted in 2011 by former Federal Election Commission chairman Trevor Potter in consultation with dozens of strategists, democracy reform leaders and constitutional attorneys from across the political spectrum.

It is supported by reform organizations such as Represent.Us, which advocate for the passage of local, state, and federal laws modeled after the AACA. It is designed to limit or outlaw practices perceived to be major contributors to political corruption.

Its provisions cover three areas:[I]

- *Stop political bribery* by overhauling lobbying and ethics laws
- *End secret money* by dramatically increasing transparency
- *Give every voter* a voice by creating citizen-funded elections

The AACA's authors state that its provisions are based on existing laws that have withstood court challenges, and are therefore are likely constitutional.

The Problem: What is the Problem We are solving?

Have you ever felt like the government doesn't really care what you think? Professors Martin Gilens (Princeton University) and Benjamin I. Page (Northwestern University) looked at more than 20 years' worth of data to answer this simple question:

Does the government represent the people?

Their study took data from nearly 2000 public opinion surveys and compared it to the policies that ended up becoming law. In other words, they compared what the public wanted to what the government actually did. What they found was extremely unsettling: The opinions of 90% of Americans have essentially no impact at all.

Tell me about the Princeton University Study

Princeton University study: Public opinion has "near-zero" impact on U.S. law. Gilens & Page found that the number of Americans for or against any idea has no impact on the likelihood that Congress will make it law. "The preferences of the average American appear to have only a miniscule, near-zero, statistically non-significant impact upon public policy.

Name one thing that does have an influence? **Money.** While the opinions of the bottom 90% of income earners in America have a "statistically non-significant impact," economic elites, business interests, and people who can afford lobbyists still carry major influence.

Nearly every issue we face as a nation is caught in the grip of corruption. Check out this slide:

10-YEAR SPENDING TO INFLUENCE U.S. GOVERNMENT, BY INDUSTRY

PHARMACEUTICAL $2.16 BIL.

ENERGY $2.93 BIL.

DEFENSE $1.26 BIL.

FINANCE $4.29 BIL.

AGRIBUSINESS $1.21 BIL.

COMMUNICATIONS $3.50 BIL.

From taxation to national debt, education to the economy,

America is struggling to address our most serious issues. Moneyed interests get what they want, and the rest of us pay the price. They spend billions influencing America's government. We give them trillions in return.

$4 Trillion

$5.8 Billion

SPENT INFLUENCING GOVERNMENT

TAXPAYER SUBSIDIES + SUPPORT

200 most politically active companies in America cash in influence.

Lobbying Pays off Big Time

In the last 5 years alone, the 200 most politically active companies in the U.S. spent $5.8 billion influencing our government with lobbying and campaign contributions.

Those same companies got $4.4 trillion in taxpayer support – earning a return of 750 times their investment. It's a vicious cycle of legalized corruption. With the help of individuals across the country, this type of activity can be made illegal.

Campaign costs are way too much in order to expect honest elections

As the cost of winning elections continues to explode, politicians of both political parties have become ever more dependent on the tiny slice of the population who can bankroll their campaigns. The rest of the population—which includes you and I—does not matter a dime.

Look at what it costs to become a US Senator. To win a Senate seat in 2014, for example, candidates had to raise $14,351 every single day. Just .05% of Americans donate more than $10,000 in any election, so it's perfectly clear who candidates will turn to first, and who they're indebted to when they win.

In return for campaign donations, elected officials pass laws that are good for their mega-donors, and bad for the rest of us. Before this expose, we may have wondered why Congress does nothing that the people want. Now it is patently obvious.

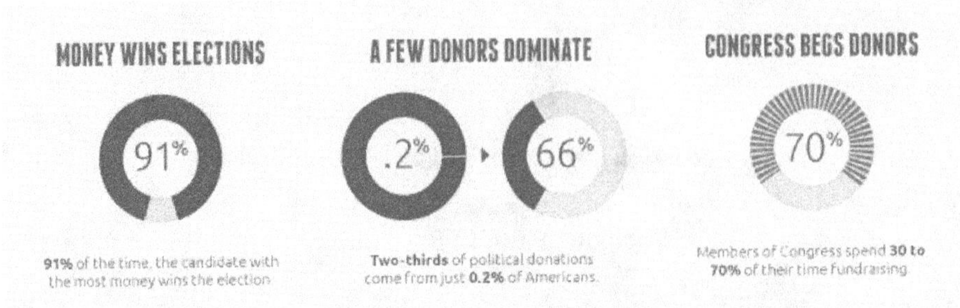

Too much time on fund raising

Our elected officials spend 30-70% of their time in office fundraising for the next election. When they're not fundraising, they have no choice but to make sure the laws they pass keep their major donors happy – or they won't be able to run in the next election. It is a vicious cycle and those who are in office more than one term are guilty of taking money for their campaigns. It ought to be against the law. Until this issue is properly addressed, corruption will continue to block progress on every issue.

Represent.Us has a plan to tackle corruption, and it's already winning:

SOURCES for information in this chapter.

Gilens and Page, "Testing Theories of American Politics: Elites, Interest Groups, and Average Citizens," Perspective on Politics, 2014.
Washington Post, "Rich People Rule!" 2014.
Washington Post, "Once again, U.S. has most expensive, least effective health care system in survey," 2014.
Forbes Opinion, "The tax code is a hopeless complex, economy-suffocating mess," 2013.
CNN, "Americans pay more for slower Internet," 2014.
The Hill, "Sanders requests DOD meeting over wasteful spending," 2015.
CBS News, "Waste book 2014: Government's questionable spending," 2014.
The Heritage Foundation, Budget Book, 2015.
The Atlantic, "American schools vs. the world: expensive, unequal, bad at math," 2013.
CNN Opinion, "War on drugs a trillion-dollar failure," 2012.
Feeding America, Child Hunger Fact Sheet, 2014.
New York Times, "Banks' lobbyists help in drafting financial bills," 2014.
New York Times, "Wall Street seeks to tuck Dodd-Frank changes in budget bill," 2014
Sunlight Foundation, "Fixed Fortunes: Biggest corporate political interests spend billions, get trillions," 2014.
Sunlight Foundation, Fixed Fortunes database, 2015.

LEARN ABOUT THE SOLUTION

The Solution

Let's take a look at the specifics precepts of the American Anti-Corruption Act:

America's corrupt political system is a complex problem. The American Anti-Corruption Act is a comprehensive solution.

Three Prong Attack AACA

The American Anti-Corruption Act sets a standard for city, state and federal laws that break big money's grip on politics. It will:

Stop political bribery by making it illegal for lobbyists to lobby a politician and donate to their campaign. You can lobby, or you can donate, but you can't do both.

End secret money so Americans know who is buying political power.

Fix our broken elections so the people, not the political establishment, are the ones in control.

Together, Represent.US we're building a nationwide movement to fix corruption. Details of the AACA follow:

No Taxation Without Representation

In communities across America, represent.Us members – conservatives, progressives and everyone in between – are working together to pass local Anti-Corruption Acts. Member-led Represent.Us chapters are leading the fight to protect our communities from the corruption that plagues Congress. In 2016, Represent.Us members passed the first statewide Anti-Corruption Act in South Dakota.

A collage about represent.us action events

Every town, city, state, and county has a unique political makeup, so every Anti-Corruption Act is uniquely tailored to the needs of each community. We can call this local action for national political power.

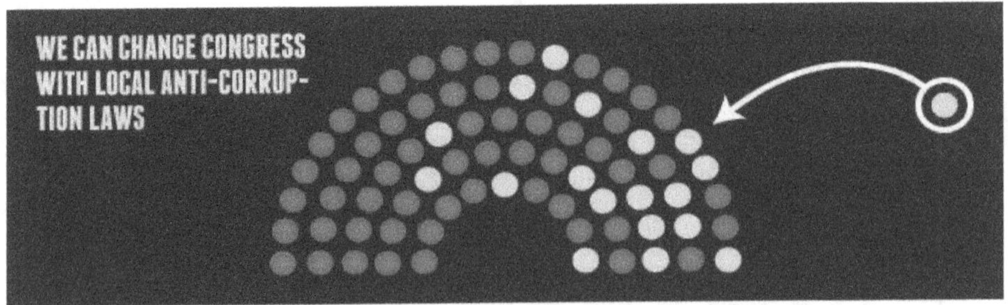

Local wins can eventually help replace a bad Congress

Every municipal and state Anti-Corruption Act creates common-sense ethics, conflict-of-interest, transparency, and campaign finance laws. State Acts create the opportunity for federal candidates from that state to campaign on the anti-corruption platform – accountable to their constituents, not special interests.

Candidates who win election on this platform have a built-in incentive to champion Anti-Corruption laws in Washington, D.C. (because that's what got them elected). Every state we win gets us one crucial step closer to passing the American Anti-Corruption Act in the federal government.

The model solution components of the American Anti-Corruption Act, are shown immediately below

THE AMERICAN ANTI-CORRUPTION ACT

The Anti-Corruption Act sets a standard for local, state and federal laws that Fix our broken elections, Stop political bribery and End secret money.

1) Fix our broken elections:

Let voters rank their top candidates: Under the Act, voters are able to rank their top candidates, allowing them to support their top choice without fear of inadvertently helping elect the other party's candidate. This makes it easier to elect independent-minded candidates who aren't beholden to establishment special interests.

End gerrymandering: The Anti-Corruption Act ends gerrymandering by creating independent, fully transparent redistricting commissions that follow strict guidelines to ensure accurate representation for all voters, regardless of political party.

Automatic voter registration: Our voter rolls and registration systems are outdated, error-prone, and costly. New and proven systems can save taxpayer money and ensure that all eligible voters are able to participate on Election Day. Automatic voter registration means all interested eligible voters can be registered when they interact with government agencies – at the DMV, getting a hunting license, applying for food assistance, or signing up for the national guard.

Let all voters participate in open primaries: The Act makes all candidates for the same office compete in a single, open primary controlled by voters, not the political establishment. This gives voters more control over our elections and more choices at the ballot.

Change how elections are funded: The Act offers every voter a small credit they can use to make a political donation with no out-of-pocket expense. Candidates and political groups are only eligible to receive these credits if they agree to fundraise solely from small donors.

The Act also empowers political action committees that only take donations from small donors, giving everyday people a stronger voice in our elections.

2) Stop political bribery:

Make it illegal for politicians to take money from lobbyists: Under the American Anti-Corruption Act, people who get paid to lobby cannot donate to politicians.

Ban lobbyist bundling: The Act prohibits lobbyists from bundling contributions.
Close the revolving door. The Act stops elected representatives and senior staff from selling off their government power for high-paying lobbying jobs, prohibits them from negotiating jobs while in office, and bars them from paid lobbying activity for several years once they leave.

Prevent politicians from fundraising during working hours: Under the Act, politicians are prevented from raising money during the workday, when they should be serving their constituents.

3) End secret money:

Immediately disclose political money online: The Anti-Corruption Act ensures that all significant political fundraising and spending is immediately disclosed online and made easily accessible to the public.

Stop donors from hiding behind secret-money groups: Under the Act, any organization that spends meaningful funds on political advertisements is required to file a timely online report disclosing its major donors.

Corruption and Book Summary

Knowing our rights in America is one of the major ways that citizens have to fight corruption. The people in other countries do not have the plethora of rights as US citizens expounded in the US Bill of Rights.

Nonetheless, there is corruption everywhere in government. It is a universal problem. It is now universally accepted that corruption poses critical challenges to economic and social development, and diverts resources from legitimate causes beneficial to society at large.

Corruption also restricts millions of people on a daily basis in their enjoyment of human rights and fundamental freedoms, contributing to the perpetuation of poverty and hindering economic opportunity.

The collective recognition of the challenges posed by endemic corruption has led to political upheaval and, in some cases, revolution as social groups disadvantaged by corruption demand accountability from their governments and public officials.

It would not be unusual action for the citizens of the US, who have already crossed the line by electing Donald Trump as President Trump was a product of citizens who could not take it anymore, hearing the call and voting to repair the system. My advice is to keep at it and do not take no for an answer from the scalawags in our own neighborhoods who claim to represent us. We can do much better.

LETS GO PUBLISH! Books by Brian Kelly

(Sold at www.bookhawkers.com; Amazon.com, and Kindle.).

The Founding of America From pre-Columbus to the post-revolutionary period.
Winning Back America: The play by play recommendation to steal the country from bad politicos
Great Players in Army Football Great Army Football played by great players..
Great Coaches in Army Football Army's coaches are all great.
Great Moments in Army Football Army Football at its best.
Great Moments in Florida Gators Football **Gators** Football from the start. This is the book.
Great Moments in Clemson Football CU Football at its best. This is the book.
Great Moments in Florida Gators Football Gators Football from the start. This is the book. **The Constitution Companion.** A Guide to Reading and Comprehending the Constitution
The Constitution by Hamilton, Jefferson, & Madison – Big type and in English
PATERNO: The Dark Days After Win # 409. Sky began to fall within days of win # 409.
JoePa 409 Victories: Say No More! Winningest Division I-A football coach ever
American College Football: The Beginning From before day one football was played.
Great Coaches in Alabama Football Challenging the coaches of every other program!
Great Coaches in Penn State Football the Best Coaches in PSU's football program
Great Players in Penn State Football The best players in PSU's football program
Great Players in Notre Dame Football The best players in ND's football program
Great Coaches in Notre Dame Football The best coaches in any football program
President Donald J. Trump, Master Builder: Solving the Student Debt Crisis!
President Donald J. Trump, Master Builder: It's Time for Seniors to Get a Break!
President Donald J. Trump, Master Builder: Healthcare & Welfare Accountability
President Donald J. Trump, Master Builder: "Make America Great Again"
President Donald J. Trump, Master Builder: The Annual Guest Plan
Great Players in Alabama Football from Quarterbacks to offensive Linemen Greats!
Great Moments in Alabama Football AU Football from the start. This is the book.
Great Moments in Penn State Football PSU Football, start--games, coaches, players,
Great Moments in Notre Dame Football ND Football, start, games, coaches, players
Four Dollars & Sixty-Two Cents—A Christmas Story That Will Warm Your Heart!
My Red Hat Keeps Me on The Ground. Darraggh's Red Hat is magical
Seniors, Social Security & the Minimum Wage. Things seniors need to know.
How to Write Your First Book and Publish It with CreateSpace
The US Immigration Fix--It's all in here. Finally, an answer.
I had a Dream IBM Could be #1 Again The title is self-explanatory
WineDiets.Com Presents The Wine Diet Learn how to lose weight while having fun.
Wilkes-Barre, PA; Return to Glory Wilkes-Barre City's return to glory
Geoffrey Parsons' Epoch... The Land of Fair Play Better than the original.
The Bill of Rights 4 Dummmies! This is the best book to learn about your rights.
Sol Bloom's Epoch ...Story of the Constitution The best book to learn the Constitution
America 4 Dummmies! All Americans should read to learn about this great country.
The Electoral College 4 Dummmies! How does it really work?
The All-Everything Machine Story about IBM's finest computer server.

Brian has written 1276 books. Others can be found at amazon.com/author/brianwkelly

www.ingramcontent.com/pod-product-compliance
Lightning Source LLC
Chambersburg PA
CBHW060844280326
41934CB00007B/913

* 9 7 8 1 9 4 7 4 0 2 1 1 9 *